D1631526

TORY BLUES

A CARTOON HISTORY OF THE CONSERVATIVE PARTY

ALAN MUMFORD

The
Political
Cartoon
Society

This edition first published in Great Britain in 2008 by the Political Cartoon Society.

Copyright © Alan Mumford and the Political Cartoon Society 2008

© Foreword Rt Hon Lord Baker of Dorking 2008

The right of Alan Mumford to be identified as Author of this Work has been asserted by him in accordance with the Copyright, Designs and Patents Act 1988.

ISBN 0-9549008-9-8

British Library Cataloguing in Publication Data

A CIP catalogue record for this book can be obtained from the British Library.

All rights reserved; no part of this publication may be reproduced, stored in a retrieval system, or transmitted in any form or by any means, electronic, mechanical, photocopying, recording, or otherwise without either the prior written permission of the Publishers or a licence permitting restricted copying in the United Kingdom issued by the Copyright Licensing Agency Ltd, 90 Tottenham Court Road, London W1P 0LP. This book may not be lent, resold, hired out or otherwise disposed of by way of trade in any form of binding or cover other than that in which it is published, without the prior consent of the Publishers.

Book design by Bruce Nivison

Cover cartoon by Chris Riddell

Printed and bound in Great Britain by Cromwell Press

CONTENTS

Acknowledgements and Copyright   5

Preface   6

Foreword by Rt Hon Lord Baker of Dorking   7

1   The Conservative Party, Press Barons and Cartoonists   9

2   Politicians Bare the Scars   21

3   From Peel to Disraeli 1832–1880   39

4   Conservatives and Liberal Unionists 1880–1902   49

5   Splits and Coalitions 1902–1922   59

6   The Natural Party of Government 1923–1945   71

7   Conservatism Redefined? 1945–1964   85

8   Conservatives Lose Their Way 1965–1976   97

9   New Conservatism Before New Labour 1976–1990   107

10   Unexpected Success to Prolonged Failure 1990–Present   119

11   Seeing Them Differently   131

12   Personalities   161

Bibliography   175

OTHER BOOKS PUBLISHED BY THE POLITICAL CARTOON SOCIETY

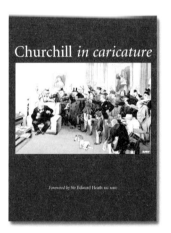

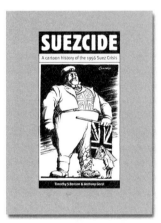

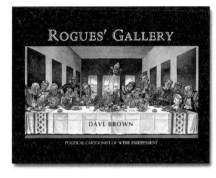

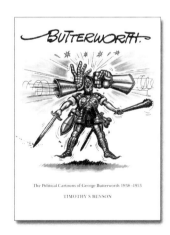

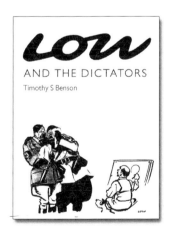

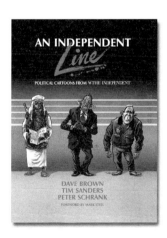

32 Store Street, London WC1E 7BS, 020 7580 1114

www.politicalcartoon.co.uk

ACKNOWLEDGEMENTS AND COPYRIGHT

The idea for this book, a companion volume to *Did Cowards Flinch*, came from Tim Benson of the Political Cartoon Society, which provided the funds for publication.

I would like to thank Geoff Fordham, Joyce Walker and Julie Reichman for proofreading the manuscript.

Helpful comments were received from Jane Barder and Colin Seymour Ure.

Special thanks to John Jensen for his identification of the cartoon by Ruby Lind.

Some early cartoons are out of copyright. We acknowledge with gratitude approval for publication from cartoonist copyright holders:
Steve Bell, Peter Brookes, Dave Brown, Andy Davey, Wally Fawkes, Nick Garland, Dave Gaskill, Les Gibbard, Charles Griffin, Ted Harrison, John Jensen, Kevin Kallaugher, Morten Morland, Chris Riddell, Martin Rowson, Gerald Scarfe, Peter Schrank, John Springs, Ralph Steadman, Martyn Turner, Keith Waite.

Approval for publication was also received from other copyright holders:
Express Newspapers for Cummings, Strube, Morning Star for Eccles, Gabriel. *Private Eye* for John Kent. Solo syndication for Cumberworth, Emmwood, IIlingworth, Jak, Low, Poy, Ridgeway, Wyndham Robinson, Vicky. *Yorkshire Evening Post* for Middleton,Telegraph Media Group for J Reynolds, Trinity Mirror for McLachlan, Vicky. Adam Birdsall, Tessa Papas, Syliva Philpin Jones, Estate of George Butterworth, Estate of Ralph Sallon, Trustees for the children of Mark Boxer.

Grateful acknowledgement is given to the following for their contribution to Chapter 2 – Politicians Bare the Scars:
Rt Hon Lord Carrington, Rt Hon Kenneth Clarke MP, Rt Hon John Gummer MP, Rt Hon Lord Heseltine, Rt Hon Michael Howard MP, Rt Hon Lord Howe, Rt Hon Lord Parkinson, Rt Hon Lord Tebbit, Rt Hon Lord Walker, Rt Hon Ann Widdecombe MP.

PREFACE

This is a companion volume to *Did Cowards Flinch*: A cartoon history of the Labour Party published by the Political Cartoon Society in 2006. It is a convention in the House of Commons that when Members have a personal, often financial, interest in a subject under discussion, they reveal that fact. The equivalent here is that I declare myself to be a member of the Labour Party. Certainly the books I have read about unemployment in the 1930's, Suez in 1956, the Thatcher revolution, have reminded me of the strongly antagonistic feelings I developed about the Conservative Party.

The choice of cartoons has depended generally on my judgement of the quality of cartoon in relation to a significant event, the availability of a good reproduction, avoidance in almost every case of cartoons which have frequently been seen elsewhere, and the fact that not all owners of syndication rights were willing to allow their cartoons to be reproduced.

The cartoons are most often critical because very few celebratory or congratulatory cartoons are good. One aspect of selection is that, apart from the Profumo Affair, I have excluded scandals. Thus cartoons on the likes of Archer, Aitken, Mellor, and Hamilton do not appear. Cartoons on them were less of a priority than cartoons on more significant issues. There are fewer cartoons on General Elections from 1945 to 1997 since they are available in my book *Stabbed in the Front* published in 2001.

This is a political history, with no attempt to deal with social and cultural events. Moreover it is largely politics as conducted at Westminster.

Alan Mumford

FOREWORD BY KENNETH BAKER, LORD BAKER OF DORKING CH

I was delighted to encourage Alan Mumford when he produced his first collection of cartoons on post-war General Elections. For those of us who are supporters of the Conservative Party this new collection together with Alan's comments in the text will probably make some wince, but that is the essence of political cartoons.

The changes of style represented in this book are fascinating. Victorian England saw the end of 18th century savagery in cartooning with all politicians becoming recognisable and barely caricatured. The only exception was Disraeli as several cartoonists exaggerated his Jewish looks, depicting him as Fagin and Shylock, and once as a lady with Jewish sideburns and long nose. The most famous cartoon of Disraeli showed him as a spiv trader in a Hampstead Heath suit, celebrating his purchase of the Suez Canal with his finger to his nose while the Sphinx gave him a wink. Cartoons like this would not be published today.

The press became sharper again towards the end of the 19th century. Beerbohm depicted Balfour as a willowy figure in the shape of a question mark – not entirely unfair as the Prime Minister's principal publication was 'A Defence of Philosophic Doubt'. During the interwar years the Tory appeasers, Baldwin and Chamberlain, were mercilessly ridiculed by the great David Low, but when Chamberlain came back from Munich fluttering his famous piece of paper, Leslie Illingworth in *Punch* depicted him as the angel of peace descending from heaven to the strains of the popular song, 'God Bless You, Mr Chamberlain'. Churchill, on the other hand, had an easy time with the cartoonists, as they loved his exuberance: his cigars, the vast range of hats, and a clever capacity to be present at critical moments – the Sidney Street Siege, the trenches in the First World War, and landing on the beaches of Normandy. However, he did not have such an effortless ride during his second premiership, when he disliked being depicted as an old man occasionally slightly out of focus. Churchill died before the wave of satire began to roll in the 1960s.

One Tory Prime Minister who was especially helped by cartoonists was Harold Macmillan. Vicky, a refugee from Hungary and a radical cartoonist, wanted to ridicule this extraordinary leftover from Edwardian England and so he depicted Macmillan in a superman costume, which was meant to make him a laughing stock. When the phrase 'SuperMac' got out into circulation it had exactly the reverse effect, for it confirmed the ease in which he overcame the Leader of the Opposition, Hugh Gaitskell. 'SuperMac' became 'SuperMan' and Macmillan increased the majority in the 1959 election.

Ted Heath was somewhat roughly treated – the woodenness, the heaving shoulders and the sharp, pointed nose. The most devastating cartoon was one by Wally Fawkes 'Trog' that showed Heath removing the grinning, laughing mask only to reveal the cold face of a very lonely man.

Nick Garland
Daily Telegraph
12 October 1989
Kenneth Baker, who owns the
original of this cartoon, got
Margaret Thatcher to sign it as
one can see.

"CARRY YOUR BAG MISSIS,"

Margaret Thatcher barely bothered to look at her caricatures. None, in her view, could ever persuade the muse of history to depict her other than what she was: a determined and successful leader who transformed her country. 'The only man in her Cabinet', 'the Iron Lady', 'the Lady's not for turning', 'she wears long skirts in order to hide her balls', all served to enhance her reputation.

John Major got it in the neck, or rather the crotch as Steve Bell in The *Guardian,* after he had discovered that John Major tucked his shirt into his underpants, made those underpants the Prime Minister's symbol. John Major was always depicted wearing naff aertex underpants over his trousers, used at times as a parachute, shopping bag or door mat. I think John Major felt victimised by these cartoons, which he saw as treating him unfairly, but cartoonists have never been too overwhelmed by fairness.

As for David Cameron, it is too early to say. Cartoonists prefer older people with 'lived-in' faces, awkward shapes and funny little mannerisms. Blair eluded them for a long time but then they settled on his teeth, ears and manic eyes. They don't quite know how to depict Cameron's blandness and good looks. An early cartoon by Peter Brookes was very flattering. It appeared during the Tory Party leadership campaign when Cameron was refusing to answer questions on whether he had taken drugs. The press, and particularly the tabloids, demanded an answer but he would not budge. He did not seek refuge as George W. Bush had done by saying that he had tried lots of things when he was young. Brookes, impressed by this resilience, drew Cameron as Gainsborough's Blue Boy standing upright in the middle of the cartoon with all the ink-splats missing him. I told David Cameron that it doesn't come better than this!

CHAPTER 1

THE CONSERVATIVE PARTY, PRESS BARONS AND CARTOONISTS

THE CONSERVATIVE PARTY

In the 18th century two groups – Whigs and Tories – dominated parliamentary politics. Their political differences dated back to the political settlement at the end of the 17th century: they were not political parties in a modern sense. Parliamentary life and power revolved around family groups and personal loyalties, with frequent intervention by the monarch in the choice of the individual to lead the government. In the 1820s political struggle first revolved around Catholic Emancipation and then Parliamentary Reform. The Duke of Wellington as Tory Prime Minister since 1828 was initially totally opposed to any reform of the almost wholly unrepresentative parliamentary constituencies, a tiny minority of the population dominated by landed gentry having the right to participate in elections. Under pressure from increasingly violent supporters of reform, he eventually gave way. The Reform Act of 1832 was passed by the Whig government, with Wellington and the Tory Peers abstaining to allow its passage.

Iain Macleod had used the word 'Tory', for example in the 1960s, to describe a particular kind of Conservative. Sometimes it is used as an alternative generic description for Conservative as it is in this book. The Tamworth Manifesto published by Sir Robert Peel in 1834 (see Chapter 3) is most often taken as the starting point of a Conservative Party. Before then there were Conservatives but there was no party. The Party was very quickly riven by the dispute over the Corn Laws (see Chapter 3) that led to a division within the Conservative Party between Peelites and Anti-Peelites, a division which was never healed as many Peelites eventually disappeared into the new Liberal Party.

Otherwise the history of the Conservative Party has been one of acquiring groups from the Liberal Party, who associated themselves with the Conservative Party and were then absorbed within it. The Liberal Unionists first supported the Conservatives in 1886 and joined the Conservative Government in 1895. Their leader Joseph Chamberlain, having broken up the Liberal Party, almost did the same to the Conservatives. The Liberal Unionists ceased to be even notionally independent in 1912 and by then had effectively been merged with the Conservatives as a Unionist Party, focused on retaining the political Union of Great Britain and Ireland. Similarly, those Liberals who joined the National government in 1931 disappeared as even a notional party in 1949.

Although important members of the Asquith and Lloyd George Coalitions in prosecuting the war from 1915 to 1918, the Conservatives retained their separate identity. They continued to do so after the 1918 General Election. Lloyd George's Coalition Government was supported by about 350 Conservatives, the Liberals in the Government having only 130 seats. I have not regarded this as essentially a Conservative Government despite this predominance of votes and, indeed, policies. However, the 1931 National Government following the 1931 General Election was hugely Conservative in membership and in Conservative support in the House of Commons. There were 471 Conservatives, 13 National Labour, and 68 Liberals – half of whom soon ceased to support the National Government.

Despite the arguments of R Bassett in his book *1931: Political Crisis*, I have treated this as a Conservative government – it walked like a duck, it quacked like a duck – it was a duck. The Churchill government from 1940 to 1945 was a genuine coalition of all three major parties.

POLITICAL THEMES

During the 19th century membership of political parties was more fluid and individuals were less likely than now always to vote for their party. Religion, Ireland and Free Trade were themes that continued to arouse great passions into the 20th century. Capacity to enthuse or influence MPs through speeches in the House of Commons mattered, so the focus of cartoons differed.

HOW IMPORTANT ARE POLITICAL CARTOONS?

Material already available in *Did Cowards Flinch* (published by the Political Cartoon Society) is not repeated here. Since the question of the influence exercised generally by newspapers on readers is difficult to answer it is not surprising that there is very little available on whether cartoons influence readers. The following chapter *Politicians Bare The Scars* presents the views of some politicians on this question. Another example to be found is the extent to which retained images of politicians feature cartoons, Churchill with a cigar or as a bulldog, Macmillan as 'SuperMac', Margaret Thatcher as the 'Iron Lady' – perhaps wielding her handbag. Supermac turned out not to be the destructive cartoon Vicky ironically intended. Perhaps the most destructive modern image has been that of Steve Bell portraying John Major as a 'super-nerd' wearing his aertex underpants outside his trousers.

There are two features of cartoons of prominent politicians worth noting here. The first is that a cartoonist's created image is constantly repeated by him, and occasionally copied by others, so that the image is fixed in the mind of the reader. The second aspect is the characteristic of a cartoon as a visual presentation, which probably relates to a different part of the brain than the written word. Specifically, cartoons deal in emotions rather than the rational aspect of our brains. The image does fix itself in our head, to the extent that it is sometimes a surprise to see the real person on television. Ted Heath's eyes and nose were nothing like the cartoonists' portrayal of them any more than Margaret Thatcher's nose was as elongated and weapon-like as it was drawn. I have found no direct comment by Harold Macmillan on his portrayal by Vicky as either SuperMac or the Entertainer. Vicky instead made the comment for him as shown in the cartoon overleaf.

FROM PRINTS TO NEWSPAPERS

The new Conservative Party was fortunate that at its founding the robust and often scatological prints of the 18th century by Gillray, Rowlandson and others had been replaced by the much more genteel prints of HB (John Doyle). Nor was there any great change except in improved quality with the arrival in 1841 of

Victor Weisz 'Vicky'
Evening Standard
15 January 1959

"YER SEE, I'M JUST AN ORDINARY BLOKE — ALL THAT SUPERMAC STUFF'S ONLY AN INVENTION BY THAT CARTOONIST FELLER.,,

Punch, the first satirical magazine in this country. Prints disappeared to a large extent and *Punch* and its relatively minor rivals, *Judy* and *Fun*, held the field for political cartoonists and especially for John Tenniel. The first daily newspaper to publish regular political cartoons was the *Pall Mall Gazette*, a London evening paper, in 1883. Francis Carruthers Gould was the first staff cartoonist on that newspaper, and later on the London *Westminster Gazette*. Like *Punch*, and *Vanity Fair*, which produced large prints of individual people, these were small circulation publications. Early on in the 20th century popular papers such as the *Daily Mail, Daily Express* and *Daily Mirror* – with huge circulations after 1918 – introduced political cartoons. Although Abu appeared in the *Observer* from 1956, the quality broadsheets generally did not have political cartoons until the 1960s (the *Morning Post* had cartoons in the 1930s and at the same time the *Manchester Guardian* reprinted Low's cartoons for the *Evening Standard*). In recent years there has been a further change. Popular papers such as the *Mirror* and *Express* no longer print cartoons five days a week. The *Evening Standard*, home of David Low for 23 years and later of Vicky and JAK no longer has cartoons at all.

As well as in published collections of their work, cartoonists like Will Dyson and David Low appeared in political posters. The work of cartoonists appeared in postcard form at the beginning of the 20th century. The arrival of television gave further opportunities for cartoonists such as Timothy Birdsall and later Les Gibbard to work directly on political programmes. Ralph Steadman drew a cartoon of Margaret Thatcher reproduced on a beer mat, which also led to the cartoon by JAK.

Ralph Steadman
January 1977

"I say, Denis, have you seen this awful drawing of me?"

Raymond Jackson 'JAK'
Evening Standard
31 January 1980

Nick Garland
Spectator
1 November 1995

FREEDOM TO DRAW OR FREEDOM TO PUBLISH?

Low was probably the first cartoonist to have a contract, which gave him largely unrestricted freedom to draw. Tim Benson found in his PhD thesis on Low and Beaverbrook that at least 40 Low cartoons were not published, largely because they were even more than usual outside the editorial preferences of the *Evening Standard*. Direct intervention of that kind seems rare now. The constraints on the cartoonists' freedom follow general questions of taste and more is acceptable now than used to be the case. Garland's cartoon of Margaret Thatcher was vetoed by the editor of the *Daily Telegraph*, and subsequently published in *The Spectator* without comment or connection with the article in which it appeared. From a political point of view the constraints may be those of the editorial line of the paper. Cartoonists like Low, Vicky and Trog moved between papers in part at least in order to find a more comfortable political home. Undoubtedly some readers would have preferred that Low and Vicky represented their Conservative views – thus the cartoon by Vicky.

Victor Weisz 'Vicky'
Evening Standard
19 May 1959

"HA HA! JOLLY GOOD, M'BOY! AT LAST, A DECENT, UNBIASED ELECTION CARTOON!"

On mass circulation newspapers in particular most cartoonists have presented roughs of four or five different cartoons and allowed the editor to choose between them, to give him or her the chance of choosing the one most likely to be comfortable for himself and his readers. There may be some self-censorship – cartoonists not drawing something because they doubt that it would be acceptable to the newspaper or to its readers. Cartoons about the Arab/Israeli conflict often generate fire from readers. The editorial slant of the newspaper, usually reflecting the views of a dominating owner, may obviously influence both the choice of cartoonist and of particular cartoons. Though there were both Conservative oriented and Liberal oriented newspapers for the 19th and most of the 20th centuries, there were many fewer Labour oriented daily newspapers – indeed until 1945 only the *Daily Herald*.

On the question of taste, the area of 'political correctness' is one in which cartoonists have to be wary. An interesting observation on this is made through the accompanying cartoon by Strube. This was based on the prevalence then of black and white minstrel shows and would presumably be quite unacceptable now. Strube was essentially repeating a minstrel's image he had drawn 20 years earlier of the then Liberal Cabinet!

Sidney Strube
Daily Express
8 November 1927

THE WEST-MINSTRELS (OPEN TO-DAY).
INTERLOCUTOR BALDWIN : " After the opening chorus, gentlemen, perhaps Massa Sambo Winston will oblige us with another Economy Joke."

15

STYLE OF CARTOONS

Cartoons of the Victorian era were decorous, ponderous, restrained and often respectable. They tended towards simply recording events rather than commenting upon them. Thus it was not a surprise that John Tenniel should be the first political cartoonist to be knighted. Francis Carruthers Gould, who was knighted, but explicitly as a Liberal supporter, said he was interested in policies rather than in personalities, which were relevant only to the extent that they in some sense represented the policy. Like most British cartoonists of his time, he did not exaggerate physical characteristics. He said about himself that he drew "with vinegar not vitriol". But his cartoons were certainly more critical than the general run of contemporary *Punch* cartoons.

The first break with relatively low-key political cartoons came with Will Dyson in the small circulation Socialist *Daily Herald*. He was quite prepared to deliver cartoons that were savage in content with a slightly greater degree of physical exaggeration. David Low, though often seen at the time as a merciless critic, actually drew in a style that did not depend on physical exaggeration – and indeed in several of his books he emphasised he did not believe in the value of cartoons drawn with malice, or drawn in an especially exaggerated form.

Low and Sidney Strube were the most popular cartoonists of the 1920s and 30s, and Low's views on Strube are interesting. Low told Strube "you are too kind to everybody. No part of a satirist's job is to be pleasing." Strube responded, "I can be tough too. Watch me tomorrow." The *denouement*, according to Low, was that Strube served up a really hot cartoon on Baldwin – only to find that he got a complimentary letter from Baldwin asking for the original. Not surprisingly Baldwin preferred Strube to Low: "Strube is a gentle genius. I don't mind his attacks because he never hits below the belt. Now Low is a genius but he is evil and malicious. I cannot bear Low." (See next chapter for Churchill's comments on Low and Strube.)

Vicky was both more directly and sharply critical of politicians, and also prepared on occasion to exaggerate some physical characteristics. He upset a lot of readers of the *Evening Standard* who wrote to complain about him. Yet his cartoons are in many respects much less savage than those of Michael Cummings in the *Daily Express*, and Leslie Illingworth in the *Daily Mail* (interestingly in *Punch* Illingworth tended to show his brilliant draughtsmanship but was much less sharply critical of politicians). Cummings was seen by one of his editors as 'to the right of Attila the Hun', but bizarrely did not regard himself as a Conservative.

Although the cartoons of Cummings, Illingworth, and Vicky after 1945 were certainly 'stronger' than most cartoons in the 1920s and 30s, it was the arrival of Gerald Scarfe and Ralph Steadman that added constant large scale physical exaggeration of politicians, in the 1960s. The cartoons further on in this book show this shift and the later adoption of physical distortion by numerous other cartoonists.

THE IMPACT OF CARTOONS

The views of politicians on the impact of cartoons are given in the following chapter. A number of quotations from cartoonists appear in *Did Cowards Flinch*. Some additional comments include:

GERALD SCARFE doubts whether they actually change the course of events. "But they can prove to be a rallying point, a sort of flag around which people can assemble and say yes that's what I thought or that's the way I feel. If I can make a person look silly I'd rather do that than make them look grotesque."

PETER BROOKES "Basically it is a knee in the groin but you hope delivered with a smile on your face. I hope I change people's perception of the people that I draw."

MICHAEL CUMMINGS "I think if the cartoonist regularly draws some political figure as a wet, the steady drip will have an effect."

RALPH STEADMAN made the most devastating comment, saying that he thought cartoons were relished by politicians because it fed their egos. So from 1989 he said he would only draw politicians from their waists downwards.

MARTIN ROWSON "Political cartoons are simultaneously political assassination without the blood, and a kind of carnivalesque feast of fools cutting great men down to size, and thus in some vague, indefinable way simply making us feel better."

One issue on impact is that a number of readers apparently still see political cartoons as being essentially jocular, aiming to make them laugh. Most modern cartoonists, certainly in the broadsheets, often seem more concerned to make a strong political point than to make anyone laugh or even smile.

HOW WOULD YOU LIKE IT?

Professor Colin Seymour-Ure defined spin as "putting a tendentious interpretation on the news". This description also fits most political cartoons. How would cartoonists react if politicians were able to put 'tendentious interpretations' on their approach, and particularly physical characteristics? Unfortunately there seem to be no Conservative politicians who have been able to prove the point. James Francis Horrabin, a cartoonist of the 1930s, was a Labour MP and Ken Gill was a former leader of the draughtsmen's trades union and a keen amateur caricaturist, but there is no Conservative equivalent. There are some cartoons drawn by cartoonists of fellow cartoonists, but too few to give a good representation here.

Max Beerbohm was probably the first caricaturist to place himself regularly in his own cartoons. Low followed suit, as did Vicky. This now seems to be out of fashion amongst cartoonists, except occasionally Martin Rowson. Steve Bell appears in his strip cartoon.

David Low
Evening Standard
21 December 1929

Victor Weisz 'Vicky'
Evening Standard
30 January 1963

Victor Weisz 'Vicky'
Lilliput (1943)

On the principle that dog does not eat dog, nor would cartoonists bite the hands that feed them, it is interesting to look at cartoons of press barons. Northcliffe, who was caricatured by Max Beerbohm and Bert Thomas in magazines, also featured in newspaper cartoons; Will Dyson on the small circulation *Daily Herald* was sharply critical. The most interesting relationship is that of Lord Beaverbrook to his cartoonists. First Low, then Vicky and Cummings tended to portray Beaverbrook with a wide mouthed smile, as in the examples here by Low and Vicky. This was in fact quite uncharacteristic of both his personality and his actual facial features. George Whitelaw poses a different view, as does Vicky, in even stronger terms, but long before he was employed on the *Evening Standard*.

Lord Beaverbrook (formerly Max Aitken before he received his peerage) was a Conservative MP from 1911 to 1916, and the owner of the *Daily* and the *Sunday Express* and the *Evening Standard*. Although an opponent of Stanley Baldwin, he was generally a supporter of most Conservative causes. The area of profound disagreement however was on Empire Free Trade, where Beaverbrook and Lord Rothermere actually promoted and paid for independent candidates to stand against the Conservative candidate. Rothermere had also told Baldwin that he would only support him in a General Election if Baldwin told him precisely who his Ministers would be. Baldwin famously assaulted them in March 1931 with his accusation that they sought "power without responsibility, the prerogative of harlots through the ages". There were no cartoons related to this speech in the *Daily Mail*, *Daily Express* or *Evening Standard*! The Cumberworth cartoon was a mild reaction. Low was generally prevented from portraying Rothermere as he wanted to. Beaverbrook had always claimed that Low had total independence (although as shown he did not) when politicians complained to him about Low's cartoons. However, Low did receive a letter from Beaverbrook describing his work as "brilliant in drawing inexhaustible in invention – and, mostly wrong in view point".

George Whitelaw
John Bull
18 January 1930

DON QUIXOTEBROOK AND SANCHO PANZAMERE

Cumberworth
News Chronicle
18 March 1939

Shepherd Baldwin guards the Conservative sheepfold.
—A Cumberworth impression.

CHAPTER 2

POLITICIANS BARE THE SCARS

A LAMB AND A WOLF

On 12 June 1901, a banquet was held in London in honour of Sir John Tenniel, who was retiring after 50 years as the main political cartoonist for *Punch*. Arthur Balfour, Leader of the House of Commons and about to become Prime Minister, gave the main speech honouring Tenniel. He felt, he said, as if he were "a proverbial lamb" proposing the "toast of the wolf on his retirement after a long and honourable career of destruction". The dinner was attended by a large number of politicians, artists and theatrical people; clearly Tenniel was much esteemed – he was the first cartoonist to have been knighted (in 1893). Gillray and Rowlandson would no doubt have been astonished by either of these distinctions. It is not easy to place oneself in the shoes of the politicians so frequently drawn by Tenniel, but from today's perspective his cartoons seem unlikely to have been felt as very hurtful by those cartooned.

Whatever damage is done by the original cartoon may be repeated. Gillray and Rowlandson were many years in their coffins before collections of their works appeared. Tenniel was the first to have several books of his cartoons published in his lifetime. The cartoons of the first staff political cartoonist, Francis Carruthers Gould later frequently reappeared in books, as were those of later cartoonists Strube, Low, Vicky and Scarfe.

Political cartoons are aimed primarily at readers who are interested in politics. But there is a subset of readers – politicians. Cartoons since 1945 have increasingly been drawn as a direct attack on politicians, not just on their policies or the values and beliefs they represent, but also on their physical appearance. Evidence on the impact of cartoons can be seen in the number and type of cartoons used in biographies and autobiographies, and from comments made by politicians.

CARTOONS IN BOOKS

Caricatures of politicians and their activities in the 18th century appeared as either coloured or black and white prints. At the birth of the Conservative Party these were still the main medium, although drawings by HB were soft in both tone and content. The arrival of *Punch* as a more or less satirical magazine in 1841 provided a base for political caricature – or, as it increasingly became called, political cartoons. Cartoons from *Punch* by Tenniel appeared in a collection on Disraeli in 1878, two years before he retired. Another Conservative to be so honoured was Winston Churchill: *A Cartoon Biography* was published in March 1955. *Punch* also provided the cartoon material for a number of volumes reporting on the activities of Parliament by H W Lucy for the last 20 years of the 19th century and also for various volumes by Harry Furniss.

BIOGRAPHIES

A different aspect of the potential impact of cartoons in books is seen in the use of cartoons within biographies. The first I can find is by R B Alderson who used 12 cartoons in his 1903 biography of Arthur Balfour (political biographies were rare before this date). Winston Churchill in his filial biography of Lord Randolph used eight cartoons in his two volumes of 1906. Moneypenny and Buckle, in what is frequently called an example of a tombstone biography of Disraeli (six volumes from 1910 – 1920) used nine cartoons. Robert Blake's single volume on Disraeli in 1966 included seven, and Stanley Weintraub in his 1993 biography of Disraeli set a record by including 24. Biographies of Conservative Prime Ministers after Balfour included few cartoons until John Charmley included 15 in his part biography of Neville Chamberlain. Randolph Churchill and his successor Martin Gilbert in the multi-volume biography of Winston Churchill included very few cartoons, but there are nine in Gilbert's *Churchill: A Life*, effectively a summary of the multi-volumes. (There are none in Roy Jenkins' biography of Winston Churchill but he refers to two of the most famous, by Low and Illingworth). The most critical biography of Eden by David Carlton included six cartoons, while his successor Macmillan was portrayed in nine cartoons in Alistair Horne's two volumes. Emrys Hughes, a left wing Labour MP, produced two critical biographies of Macmillan and Alec Douglas Home, with 11 and 12 cartoons respectively – predominantly by Vicky. There are no cartoons in the most recent major biography of Margaret Thatcher by John Campbell or in Seldon's 1998 biography of John Major.

Another aspect of the treatment of politicians can be seen in three histories of the Conservative Party. There are 14 in Robert Blake's *The Conservative Party from Peel to Major*, but 49 in John Ramsden's *An Appetite for Power*. In contrast Alan Clark's *The Tories* has no cartoons – presumably Clark did not want readers to be distracted from his own witty assaults on politicians. His first comments about cartoonists in the text combine prejudice and inaccuracy. He claims "Low, Zec and Strube cartoonists, all, interestingly of East European origin." (True only for Zec.) He asserts later that Bell's portrayal of Major with his underpants outside his trousers was like Vicky's Supermac and showed Major 'still in charge'!

On the whole cartoons in all these books were primarily intended to provide illustration rather than to make a strong political point. There are very few references to cartoons in the texts, which would be needed if they were meant to make a strong political point, as the cartoon itself originally intended. So the conclusion is that the cartoons included are unlikely to cause howls of anguish or indrawn breath about the audacity of the cartoon (see especially John Charmley's book on Chamberlain for a collection of *Punch* cartoons that have the impact of a feather duster in referring to Chamberlain's failed peace policies).

AUTOBIOGRAPHIES

As with biographies, references to cartoons are very rare. Full scale autobiographies by senior Conservative politicians have appeared only in the last 50 years. Winston Churchill did not produce an autobiography, although Balfour described his book, *The World Crisis*, as "Winston's brilliant autobiography disguised as a history of the universe". There are no cartoons either in that book or the British edition of his volumes on the Second World War. R A Butler's well reviewed *The Art of the Possible* included seven cartoons, of which he owned the originals. Macmillan matched Moneypenny and Buckle by producing six volumes, but included only three cartoons. James Prior, one of Margaret Thatcher's 'Wets', produced a book unusual not because of the five cartoons he includes but because on the back cover he has a cartoon by Stanley Franklin of himself being hung out to dry by Margaret Thatcher. This degree of prominence is uncommon, as is the fact that it is not a celebration of Prior's achievements.

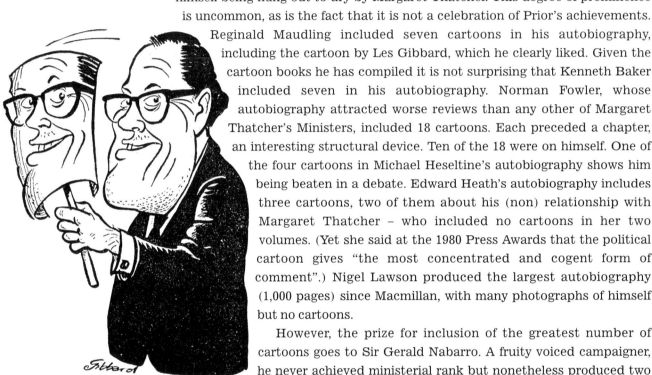

Reginald Maudling included seven cartoons in his autobiography, including the cartoon by Les Gibbard, which he clearly liked. Given the cartoon books he has compiled it is not surprising that Kenneth Baker included seven in his autobiography. Norman Fowler, whose autobiography attracted worse reviews than any other of Margaret Thatcher's Ministers, included 18 cartoons. Each preceded a chapter, an interesting structural device. Ten of the 18 were on himself. One of the four cartoons in Michael Heseltine's autobiography shows him being beaten in a debate. Edward Heath's autobiography includes three cartoons, two of them about his (non) relationship with Margaret Thatcher – who included no cartoons in her two volumes. (Yet she said at the 1980 Press Awards that the political cartoon gives "the most concentrated and cogent form of comment".) Nigel Lawson produced the largest autobiography (1,000 pages) since Macmillan, with many photographs of himself but no cartoons.

However, the prize for inclusion of the greatest number of cartoons goes to Sir Gerald Nabarro. A fruity voiced campaigner, he never achieved ministerial rank but nonetheless produced two volumes of autobiography, and in the first there were 53 cartoons – of himself. He was overcome by modesty in the second volume in which there were only 38 cartoons. Unsurprisingly the cartoons included in these and other autobiographies are generally approving, congratulatory or mildly funny – Prior and Heseltine's are exceptions.

Les Gibbard
From '*Memoirs*'
Reginald Maudling
1978

OTHER BOOKS BY CONSERVATIVES

Kenneth Baker's interest in cartoons has been expressed in four books, of which the most relevant here is his *The Prime Ministers* in which he makes the observation "the lesser figures can be hurt, particularly if they show that the attack has struck home". He has also said "politicians have a love/hate relationship with cartoonists. They love to appear in cartoons and indeed for a rising politician it is a sign he has arrived. On the other hand, they wince when the darts hit home."

Lord Birkenhead produced a book, *Contemporary Personalities*, in 1924, which included 30 cartoons to illustrate each personality. (They were by Matt, not the current *Daily Telegraph* cartoonist.) In recent years two Conservative politicians have followed Roy Jenkins' example in producing political biographies: Douglas Hurd on Robert Peel and William Hague on Pitt the Younger, both of which include cartoons.

Winston Churchill provided the most extensive comments on cartoons and cartoonists in an article for *Strand* magazine, republished in his *Thoughts and Adventures* in 1932. The tone was one of amused magnanimity, the only criticism offered was to cartoonists who he thought had made too much of his hats.

COMMENTS BY CONSERVATIVE POLITICIANS

Arthur Balfour, whose views on Tenniel appeared at the beginning of this chapter, also commented on Will Dyson, the great socialist cartoonist: "a probably dangerous young man, but at once too subtle and too violent to be greatly feared". Baldwin's vehement reaction to the cartoons of Low as compared with Strube has already been given.

Lord Birkenhead, himself a master of invective, in 1928 thanked Lord Beaverbrook, proprietor of the *Evening Standard*, for the "growing and friendly refinement of your Radical Cartoonist" – Low. He had presumably recovered from seeing Low's cartoon of him as Lord Burstinghead in 1926. In June 1929 he presented a different view to Beaverbrook. "Your cartoonist over a long period of time published filthy and disgusting cartoons of me which were intended and calculated to do me great injury". He exploded further in a later letter: "I know all about modern caricature and I never had cause for grievance until you a friend allowed a filthy little Socialist to present me daily as a crapulous and corpulent buffoon."

It is not surprising that as an active politician Churchill should have been complimentary about cartoonists. It is much more sensible for politicians not to seem to be hurt or damaged by cartoons. So in *Thoughts and Adventures* Churchill wrote "just as eels are supposed to get used to skinning so politicians get used to be being caricatured.... They even get to like it." "Low is the greatest of our modern cartoonists, the greatest because of the vividness of his political conceptions. He is the Charlie Chaplin of caricature and tragedy and comedy are the same to him." He comments on a Low cartoon of the 1924 General Election: "there is not a figure in it that is not instinct with maliciously perceived truth". The use of 'maliciously' perhaps betrays at least some ambivalence about Low, who he also described as a "green eyed young antipodean radical". He refers to the cartoons of Sidney Strube, Low's popular contemporary, as "examples of his genial spirit".

David Low
New Statesman
1926

Churchill was also often surprisingly complimentary about Low's cartoons, even when they were critical. One, on 29 January 1935, poked fun at Churchill's continued opposition to the Government's India Policy and he sent a copy to his wife saying it "should make you laugh".

But Churchill was not always prepared to accept the virtues of cartoons and cartoonists. As war time Prime Minister Churchill was frequently critical of Low, criticising him to Beaverbrook as a "communist of the Trotsky variety". After he became Prime Minister in 1940 he was very critical not only of the famous cartoon by Philip Zec ("The price of petrol has gone up") but also thought Low's Colonel Blimp was destructive of British morale. Roy Jenkins makes no comment about either issue in his biography. There is no written comment from Churchill on Low's cartoon of the two Churchills – "The leader of humanity and the party leader" on 31 July 1945. However, normal relations with Low were apparently restored when he chose him to illustrate the North American edition of his Second World War memoirs.

Churchill did express anger with another cartoonist, this time Leslie Illingworth, who in *Punch* on 3 February 1954 showed him as much aged. This was probably all the more of a shock because most cartoonists like Low, Vicky and Cummings were drawing cartoons of him which even though critical showed him as a twinkling figure. Churchill was deeply upset by Illingworth's cartoon to the extent of saying "there's malice in it..... I shall have to retire if this sort of thing goes on". But he did not retire for another year. He cannot have seen the more devastating cartoon by Gerald Scarfe of Churchill's last years in the House of Commons, eventually published in *Private Eye* on 5 February 1965, having earlier been refused by *The Times*. Churchill's public comment on the Sutherland portrait presented to him on his 80th birthday, which some people saw as a caricature, was restrained, when he said "it certainly combines force and candour".

Randolph Churchill, son of Winston, featured in a number of Low cartoons as an aspirant politician in the 1930s. His views on Low are not known but in the introduction to a collection of Vicky cartoons *Twists* in 1962 he wrote "for it is one of the endearing characteristics of Vicky that he has no victims. There is never an element of malice in the story he has to tell" – not a view all Vicky's subjects were likely to share.

In his first volume of his autobiography Gerald Nabarro wrote of Michael Cummings, "who adds vivacity and insight to every political situation he depicts", and complimented Vicky on his "perspicacity and artistry". He also said that the cheques he sent for Vicky's cartoons of him "always went to refugee or charitable organisations".

Vicky invented, as cartoonists do, his own version of Selwyn Lloyd. In Vicky's cartoons he appears as a small man with a very large nose – neither accurate depictions. But Vicky's version became the public image. Lloyd's comment about Vicky was not in words but in a drawing. He drew a cartoon of Vicky as a devil with horns, and took it along to Vicky's 50th birthday celebration.

Like Gerald Nabarro, James Prior had a view about Michael Cummings. In the introduction Prior made to Cummings' collection of cartoons *On the Point of my Pen*, he wrote: "Cummings has had a lot of fun at my expense but I have enjoyed his cartoons, which have always been prejudiced and distorted in the best traditions of the *Daily* and *Sunday Express*". The double edged nature of this "compliment" is perhaps sharpened by the fact that Cummings does not appear as one of the four cartoonists in Prior's autobiography.

The issue of malice recurs in many comments by politicians. Ted Heath wrote of Low, in the introduction to *Churchill in Caricature* (Political Cartoon Society 2005), "he lacked the malice that so often diminishes the work of contemporary cartoonists". In Heath's view "the best cartoons can bring to life the issues and conflicts of the day in a way that mere words never quite seem to manage".

"CHEER UP, YOU'RE JUST FIGMENTS OF THE IMAGINATION OF THOSE FOOLISH CARTOONIST FELLERS!"

Lord Hailsham, an ebullient figure who often concealed his intelligence in over forceful attacks on other politicians, was frequently portrayed in cartoons ringing a bell – one of the over the top manifestations of his time as Chairman of the Conservative Party. Hailsham, or Quintin Hogg as he was at various times, is the only politician I have found who attacked a cartoonist directly, as the accompanying cartoon shows. Nicholas Ridley, senior Cabinet Minister in

Victor Weisz 'Vicky'
Evening Standard
10 January 1963

Nick Garland
Spectator
12 July 1990

Margaret Thatcher's last days, had the misfortune of believing that a journalist with a tape recorder would treat their conversation over lunch as an entirely private matter. Ridley expressed worries about growing German power on 12 July 1990, and also disparaged Helmut Kohl, the then German Chancellor. Not only did the *Spectator* publish these remarks, but it highlighted them with a front page cartoon. Ridley resigned and in his autobiography complained that the cartoon "wrongly suggested that I had compared Herr Kohl to Hitler". His colleague Kenneth Baker thought this cartoon "did more damage than the article itself".

Martin Rowson
Mug shots
2005

It was John Major's misfortune to be captured in many people's eyes by Steve Bell's cartoon of him wearing his underpants outside his trousers. Major is quoted in Seldon's *Major: A Political Life* as saying that the cartoon "is intended to destabilise me and so I ignore it". Michael Portillo was one of a number of politicians drawn by Martin Rowson to decorate the walls of the Gay Hussar Restaurant in London. In the subsequent book *Mug Shots* he says of Portillo's reaction, "first of all he said the cartoon was terrible, easily the worst he had ever seen of himself. Then he said it was terrible because it was so accurate; unlike any other cartoonist, I'd caught his drooping right eyelid."

MORE OPINIONS

A number of Conservative politicians were asked for comments for this book and responded either by letter or interview. Ann Widdecombe was the only woman, of four invited, to give comments.

THE INFLUENCE OF CARTOONS

"I find political cartoons a very effective way of expressing a view about political issues. I particularly enjoy those that inject humour and, on occasion, satire into a subject. I think politicians and the media have a tendency to pontificate, and humour is a great antidote."
Lord Parkinson

"Of course political cartoons are influential. They sometimes capture the essence of the point in a devastating fashion. As to those which depict me, you will not be surprised to hear that I like some but not others!"
Michael Howard MP

"I do think that political cartoons are an essential part of our modern politics. They can even be quite influential by making a cutting political point if a cartoon strikes a thought that was already in the head of many of the newspaper readers."
Kenneth Clarke MP

Wally Fawkes 'Trog'
The Times Saturday Magazine

"One cartoon can be worth a thousand-word thesis. Some, of course, serve merely to make people laugh but most political cartoons also have a message that is usually a pungent comment on some event. Some will stand the test of time and others will be incomprehensible to future generations without a few footnotes explaining the context. For example, one of my own favourites from my personal collection is a cartoon done by Nick Garland showing Michael Portillo, William Hague and myself dancing and singing with a "little bit of blooming luck" and on the stage set is a placard suggesting that the Tories are opposing a 3 May Election. It was at the time of a revival of *My Fair Lady* on the London stage. That is not a connection that anybody looking back could make but it was worth a thousand words as to why the Tories might be opposing an early Election, despite all their rhetoric."
Ann Widdecombe MP

John Jensen
Parliamentary Sauce
compiled by Greg Knight
1993

"Cartoonists can influence the perception of people particularly if that perception is continuously reinforced. All anybody remembers about Harold Wilson is that he smoked a pipe because there was virtually no cartoon of the time in which he didn't have one. Cartoons also reinforce the perception of character; John Major was portrayed in cartoon after cartoon as weak and grey whereas those of us who knew him would say the opposite."
Ann Widdecombe MP

"Cartoons, because they can encapsulate a complex issue in a graphic and immediately understood way, can be effective and influential."
Lord Tebbit

"It is hard now to pick out particular cartoons from almost 30 years ago, but I remember a cartoon of the Liberal Leader as a post box with electors shovelling ballots into his mouth and Harold Wilson behind the box which had its door open shovelling them into a bag marked Labour. It expressed more succinctly the tactical voting issue than any amount of verbal argument."
Lord Tebbit

"Cartoons were an important part of political life, but they are having a declining impact because of the growth in TV coverage."
Lord Hurd

"I think cartoons are very effective in terms of both foreign and home affairs and party politics but, of course, it depends on whether the cartoonist managed to get it right."
Lord Carrington

"For many people visual images have more impact than text. This can be especially true with depictions repeated constantly. In his early days in politics Vicky was an example. He greatly influenced Labour and Socialist opinions."
Lord Walker

"Political cartoons are unlikely to add to political controversy but certainly do not diminish it; they are an integral part of the development of political debate. Sometimes cartoonists had a more lasting impact than other journalists, sometimes creating a particular character or role for a character. Some people had an image created for them, through the constant repetition of an original image by one or more cartoonists. In my own case a certain element of wildness had been an element of the image." Partly it was his hair flying in an uncontrolled way, partly the incident over the Mace. He remembered an episode on *Spitting Image*; as a backbencher, he was shown with a bomb under the Cabinet table. He could not remember a particularly unkind or monstrously unfair cartoon – though maybe the worst had disappeared from his memory. On the whole he thought cartoonists laughed with him.
Lord Heseltine

Lord Hurd's father and grandfather were both MPs and therefore he lived in a political context. *Punch*, politics and cartoons were a feature of particularly his early life. 'Dropping the Pilot' was one cartoon that had stayed in his memory. He 'saw' Disraeli and Gladstone through the cartoons of them, rather than photographs. Earlier, Peel would only have been known facially to most people through cartoons – he was the last Prime Minister not to be photographed.

Cartoonists he remembered strongly included Sir Bernard Partridge who drew for so many years for *Punch*, and later David Low. While late 18th century cartoonists had been very savage, for most of the 19th and up to the mid 20th century cartoonists were more moderate in their style. Low could be strongly critical without being savage. In contrast, he thought contemporary cartoonists often drew in a savage exaggerated way that for him was often not very effective. Scarfe was an example.
Lord Hurd

CARTOONS ABOUT ME...
"I have never really regarded them as more than entertainment – except when they annoy me!"
Lord Howe

Lord Hurd could not remember any savage cartoons on himself – perhaps because his political career did not involve the kind of political decisions about which cartoonists would be likely to be very savage. He felt he was more subject to mockery and being teased rather than harsher cartoons. He thought some of his colleagues were affected by cartoons, particularly by *Spitting Image*.
Lord Hurd

"As far as cartoons about myself are concerned, I have been amused far more often than irritated, and generally found them helpful rather than unhelpful."
Lord Tebbit

Lord Walker did not much mind whether cartoons on himself were pro or anti but either way he preferred that they were funny and with good humour. As with written material you had to become immune. He had received good advice as a Minister from a Conservative Backbencher when he had been violently criticised: "It will be forgotten a week later".
Lord Walker

Peter Brookes
The Times

"I have never worried too much about them; one always likes the cartoons, which are favourable, and dismisses those which are not!"
Lord Carrington

"As to cartoons about myself, my usual reaction is to laugh, and I have a good collection of them."
John Gummer MP

Lord Heseltine included cartoons in his autobiography. He said that the cartoon by Brookes was a wholly legitimate comment on an occasion when he was bested in a debate by Gordon Brown. "Perhaps it was in one sense cruel because it was

Peter Brookes
The Times

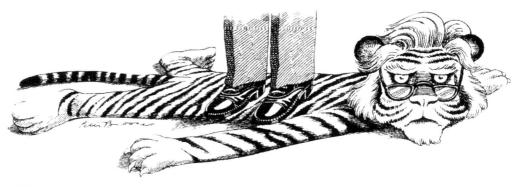

so accurate." His cartoon collection, placed up the stairs of his country home, still makes him laugh, as it does his friends when they visit. He particularly liked JAK and remembered one of his cartoons in relation to the Poll Tax and he remembered two opposing cartoons about the Mace episode. One showed Michael Foot triumphant, the other showed him as the victor in the action, as an heroic figure standing against the mob.

On the whole he thought he had been treated quite well by cartoonists. For example the image of him as Tarzan by no means diminished him, in comparison with the way in which other politicians were portrayed.
Lord Heseltine

"I have nearly always enjoyed cartoons of myself. I am particularly fond of Garland and Steve Bell cartoons. Steve Bell could never understand this and always commented with some surprise when I rang him up to tell him how much I enjoyed one of his efforts and how I would like a copy, as they were usually intended to be deeply insulting! I enjoy Peter Brookes' cartoons also because they are witty, easily recognisable caricatures and the impact is lasting rather than ephemeral. My all-time favourite of cartoons portraying myself was one done by Charles Griffin in May 1997. At the time I had said that Michael Howard had 'something of the night' about him. Most cartoonists pounced on this eagerly to portray Michael as some sort of Dracula figure but the controversy had sprung from the dismissal of the Head of the Prison Service, Derek Lewis. A few days after I had made my own comment a scurrilous article appeared in the *Daily Mail* falsely accusing me of having been wooed by Lewis with flowers and chocolate."
Ann Widdecombe MP

Charles Griffin
The Express
15 May 1997

'That's **awfully sweet of** you, Derek, but I'd rather you brought me a can of worms'

"I am a keen collector of 19th century and early 20th century cartoons and caricatures. Inevitably, therefore, I have also indulged in a form of vanity shared by several politicians and tried to collect the originals of cartoons about my own political career over the years. The distinguished collection of past statesmen hangs on the walls of our living rooms and the private collection of ones showing me is hidden from general public views in the loo and my bedroom."

"The cartoons of myself provide a very amusing souvenir of just about every wild political controversy that I have ever been involved in. I have not gone out of my way to collect flattering ones so that some still arouse a twinge of pain when I look at them. There are one or two that my wife particularly dislikes and she has jokingly threatened to destroy one by Griffin of the *Daily Mirror* after I eventually fall off the perch."
Kenneth Clarke MP

ON CARTOONISTS

"There was only one cartoonist especially significant for me, Osbert Lancaster."
Lord Hurd

On Michael Cummings: "It was death by a thousand strokes but at least I die laughing."
Lord Heseltine

"For me JAK of the *Evening Standard*, Giles of the *Express* Group and Osbert Lancaster and subsequently Matt of the *Telegraph* are or were wonderfully effective commentators on the events of the day. I am afraid brutal cartoons often seem to me too portentous and are much less effective. In spite of rumours to the contrary, most politicians have very thin skins and very few enjoy seeing themselves parodied or caricatured in cartoons and I am no exception. Once again, I exclude those that are humorous rather than cutting; JAK in particular made me laugh at myself and that again is no bad thing. I have a number of his cartoons, which I bought because I like them and although they were critical, they were not malicious."
Lord Parkinson

"I have enjoyed so many cartoonists' work, but perhaps particularly JAK's and Garland's cartoons of myself."
Lord Tebbit

"Vicky was a very influential cartoonist, and I was pleasantly surprised when Vicky did a cartoon of me early in my political career. Joseph Lee of the London *Evening News* was good and Osbert Lancaster, who was a shrewd student of politics, had enormous impact. I used to look for his cartoon and laugh. Vicky's cartoons of Macmillan as Supermac and the Entertainer turned attention away from the Edwardian image that had previously identified him. It was the cartoonist who totally changed Macmillan's image – unintentionally helpful to the Conservative Party. The actor image did capture some aspects of Macmillan."
Lord Walker

"Recently, I think there are some cartoonists in the broadsheets who seem to prefer the bludgeon and the grotesque, rather than the sword and humour. For me, my two favourite cartoonists have always been Matt in the *Daily Telegraph* and Garland, also in the *Telegraph*. In previous times, Low was absolutely superb and Vicky was not at all bad – he made a great success of Harold Macmillan."
Lord Carrington

Nick Garland
Daily Telegraph
31 March 1982

"My favourite cartoonist is actually 'Trog', who is an excellent draughtsman. I suspect that I was also influenced by the fact that he was an excellent jazz clarinettist as Wally Fawkes and he also was the cartoonist for a strip cartoon in the *Daily Mail* called 'Flook'. He plainly was never a Conservative, but he produced some very cutting commentaries on my party over the Years."
Kenneth Clark MP

"I have to say I respect Matt enormously. I hugely regret the death of Timothy Birdsall and it was when passing a blue plaque recently that I remembered again how much we have lost by the death of Vicky."
John Gummer MP

OTHER COMMENTS

"When I first started collecting cartoons people like Wally Fawkes would send me originals that I asked for in exchange for something like a bottle of brandy. Every cartoonist now realises that they can get a more serious sum of money from a politician who wants to buy a souvenir. I suppose that I should console myself with the thought that now that cartoons have acquired a value it does mean that people do now appreciate their quality more seriously."
Kenneth Clark MP

Wally Fawkes 'Trog'
The *Observer*
18 November 1979

"The Trog Marilyn Monroe cartoon illustrates dramatically how skilfully an image can be depicted with only a line or two."
Lord Howe

"One of the things which cartoonists did was to help create an image of politicians. Sometimes this was positive and popular, as with Churchill's cigar and Wilson's pipe. Sometimes of course the image was much less positive." He thought politicians were quite conscious of their image in general and probably also specifically in relation to cartoons. Cartoonists had made a lot of Margaret Thatcher's handbag, and he thought she was very conscious of her handbag – though not necessarily of cartoons.
Lord Hurd

"I do not think that women are treated any differently in cartoons from men. Obviously it depends on the caricature of the appearance but that applies to both sexes. William Hague is always bald, Michael Heseltine always had a vast bouffant of hair, Tony Blair always has bat ears, Edward Heath always had a vastly exaggerated grin and with women it is largely the same; some characteristic is picked out and shown. I often wonder what cartoonists would do these days when my old black pudding bowl hairstyle, so loved by that profession, has been exchanged for a long blonde flick."
Ann Widdecombe MP

"I particularly remember cartoons of the Macmillan Government, which was God's gift to any half competent cartoonist, and I think that cartooning and satire played a key part in the end of Macmillan's career and the fall of the Conservative Government in 1964, when I fought my first unsuccessful campaign as a Parliamentary candidate."
Kenneth Clarke MP

"I remember a Nicholas Bentley cartoon at the time at which the Liberals would adopt anyone who was famous as a parliamentary candidate, where a haughty Lady Violet Bonham-Carter was saying "No, I certainly would not support Sabrina as a Liberal candidate. (Sabrina was a well endowed female celebrity with **NO** intellectual pretensions.)"
John Gummer MP

"In my opinion, one of the key differences in temperament between people who tend to be Conservative and people who tend to be Socialists is that more Tories have a sense of humour. I have always found that too many members of the hard left are rather humourless individuals, however worthy in other ways, although there are some spectacular exceptions. Any good Tory should be able to enjoy a joke at his own expense, although I fear that Ted Heath and Margaret Thatcher were exceptions even to that rule."
Kenneth Clarke MP

CHAPTER 3

FROM PEEL TO DISRAELI

1832–1880

The term 'Conservative' as a political description was first used in Britain in 1830 in the *Quarterly Review*. It then came into more general political use without being attached initially to any particular group of people.

Sir Robert Peel was appointed Prime Minister in 1834 when William IV (the last Sovereign to take this initiative) dismissed Lord Melbourne. Peel decided that in the circumstances created by the 1832 Reform Act it was desirable before the General Election of 1835 to present to the electorate a coherent view of the principles he and his Government proposed to use. He agreed with his Cabinet a statement to his constituency known as the Tamworth Manifesto, published in the three main newspapers. Although the word Conservative does not appear in the Manifesto, it is generally agreed by historians to be the defining statement for a new Conservative Party. The Duke of Wellington and the Tories had been absolutely opposed to any significant reform or change. Peel moved from his original agreement with this position to a more pragmatic approach. There would be no attempt to reverse the 1832 Reform Act, which he "accepted as the final and irreversible settlement of a great constitutional question". However, there would be no instant redress for anything which anyone might call an abuse. There would instead be respect for deference and prescriptive authority. Yet there could be the correction of proven abuses and the redress of real grievances and no automatic opposition to reasonable change. All possibilities would be reviewed against the principles of strict Government economy.

Individuals and groups of politicians moved between parties from 1834 just as they had done previously. The first significant shift was that of Lord Edward Stanley and his colleagues, who left the Whigs in 1835. He joined the Conservative Government formed by Peel when the latter won a majority in 1841. In common with most Conservatives Peel had supported the Corn Laws, which prevented the importation of cheaper corn to this country, but he returned in 1841 with a commitment to reform them. Disraeli, who had been refused even minor office by Peel, launched pyrotechnic attacks on his leader from the back benches. Lord Stanley, saying that the Government should stick to the views of the party, led a majority of the Cabinet, and many backbenchers, opposed to changing the Corn Laws. Repeal was eventually carried by Peel's Conservative supporters (one third of the party) and the Whigs.

The split between the Peelites and the protectionists, registered with the passage of the repeal on 28 May 1846, became a significant feature of politics over the next 30 years and part of Conservative Party mythology in relation to what Peel had done – splitting the party. The majority Conservative view about him then and since has been Disraeli's 'damn your principles, stick to your party'. Peel had put little effort into persuading his party: he led and they should follow. The last Prime Minister not to be photographed, his public image came from black and white cartoons of him. His lack of personal charm was captured by an Irishman, John Philpot Curran, who said that Peel's smile illuminated his countenance "like a silver plate on a coffin".

Stanley, now the Earl of Derby, became Prime Minister of a minority Conservative Government in 1852. Disraeli, a wholly uncharacteristic

Conservative, was the Leader of the House of Commons and Chancellor of the Exchequer in a Cabinet, the majority of whose members were unknown to the Duke of Wellington: his response became the nickname for the Government – "Who? Who?"

The Peelites had not taken office under Lord Derby. Instead William Gladstone, Lord Aberdeen and other major Peelites joined the Whigs to form a government in January 1853. The formal separation was recognised in a very British way when Peelites resigned from the Conservative Carlton Club. Gladstone had declined to rejoin the Conservatives, helped to set up the new Liberal Party and from 1859 his long rivalry with Disraeli dominated politics. Their personal antagonism was reflected in Disraeli's public description of Gladstone as "a sophistical rhetorician inebriated with the exuberance of his own verbosity." In private he called him "an unprincipled maniac".

The major issue for the Conservative Party, remaining a minority through several General Elections, became its response to proposals for further parliamentary reform. Conservatives and moderate Whigs defeated Gladstone's proposals in 1864. Derby and Disraeli decided that they needed both to reduce agitation and to ditch Gladstone by introducing reform of the electoral system. Paradoxically in 1867 they had to go further than Gladstone in extending the vote more widely in order to secure benefits from the redistribution of seats. Disraeli, who had initially opposed reform, was the author of what Derby described as "a leap in the dark", which doubled the electorate and did include some working class voters, though this was not the prime objective.

In February 1868 Disraeli was appointed Prime Minister. "I have climbed to the top of the greasy pole," he said. His first experience as Prime Minster lasted only ten months because he lost the General Election in 1868. More reform of the electoral system had not produced benefits for the Conservatives. In 1872 he made a significant speech at the Crystal Palace in which in spelled out three major elements of Conservatism: maintenance of the Empire, preservation of the national institutions and elevation of the condition of the people.

The first Conservative majority in the House of Commons since 1841 came at the 1874 General Election, the first to be held through a secret ballot, reducing although not entirely eliminating the most obvious corrupt electoral practices. 1875 saw the first fruits of Disraeli's principle of "elevation of the condition of the people", with social reform in housing, easing the legal position of trades unions and the encouragement of education through tax support for church schools. In 1876 Disraeli went to the Lords as the Earl of Beaconsfield, the last sitting Prime Minister to take this step. With Salisbury his foreign secretary, at the Congress of Berlin in 1878 he produced both a settlement with Turkey that prevented a war in Europe, and allowed the acquisition of Cyprus by Britain. Yet another Disraeli statement echoed down the years to a later British Prime Minister: "Lord Salisbury and myself have brought you back peace – but a peace I hope with honour."

Punch
1845
Sir Robert Peel's Government had offended many Conservative MPs by giving grants to the Maynooth Catholic Seminary in Ireland. He was supported by the Whigs under Lord John Russell, who were dismayed when Peel donned the hat of Free Trade also, in relation to the Corn Laws.

THE MAN WOT PLAYS SEVERAL INSTRUMENTS
AT ONCE.

STAG AT BAY
HB (John Doyle)
1846
Peel is savaged here by his Conservative opponents on abolishing the Corn Laws. Lord William Bentinck is on the left, Disraeli on the right. The print is based on the painting by Sir Edwin Henry Landseer exhibited in 1846 at the Royal Academy.

Punch
29 November 1845
Sir Robert Peel is depicted at the time of discussions in Cabinet about cutting import duties on corn, following potato blight in Ireland. He is holding a standard implying support for industry – the stronger motivation rather than the famine for his proposal.

EATING THE LEEK.

FLUELLEN . . . MR. COBDEN.   PISTOL . . . MR. DISRAELI

FLUELLEN.   "*I pray you fall to; if you can mock a leek, you can eat a leek.*"—HEN. V.

☞ The Derby Ministry declared their adherence to the Free-trade Policy of Messrs. Cobden and Bright, which they had formerly resisted.—1852.

John Leech
Punch
18 November 1852
In Shakespeare's *Henry V* Fluellen addresses Pistol 'I pray you fall to; if you can mock a leek you can eat a leek'. The Free Trade leader (Richard Cobden backed by John Bright) presses the Free Trade leek on Disraeli. The Conservative Chancellor of the Exchequer adopted this policy which he had so strongly opposed in 1845.

Frederick Barnard
Fun
18 December 1869
The Marquis of Salisbury had
resigned from the Conservative
government in 1867,
disapproving the Reform Act.
Here on the left he is prepared
to contest with the new Earl of
Derby for leadership of the
party in the Lords. Disraeli the
ex-Prime Minister in the
Commons would have been
affected – but Derby survived.

AT LAST.

On the resignation of Lord Derby, Mr. Disraeli was entrusted with the task of forming a Conservative Ministry.

John Proctor
Judy
4 March 1868
Disraeli claimed in a phrase which subsequently became a political cliché 'I have climbed the top of the greasy pole' when he became Prime Minister on 27 February 1868. The upstanding Gladstone and tiny Lord John Russell are preparing to bring him down.

John Tenniel
Punch
14 May 1870
Gladstone and Disraeli are shown holding each other's books – Disraeli's novel Lothair, Gladstone's book on Greek Mythology.   A copy of *Punch* provides a third advertisement.

J Gordon Thomson
Fun
21 February 1874
Disraeli as leader of the opposition addresses his ex-Foreign Secretary Lord Derby during the General Election of 1874, over the head of Gladstone.

J Gordon Thomson
Fun
11 April 1874
The text under the cartoon gives a cynical representation of Disraeli's instruction to his Chancellor of the Exchequer, Sir Stafford Northcote, after winning the General Election in 1874.

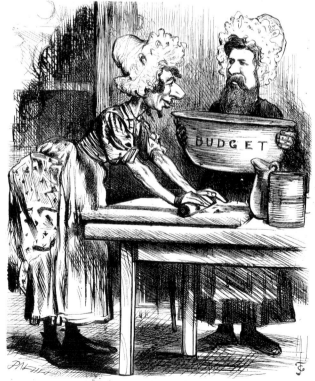

Carlo Pellegrini 'Ape'
Vanity Fair
1869
Lord Salisbury
Lord Salisbury was a violent opponent of Disraeli and the Conservative Reform Act of 1867 which he saw as a betrayal of Conservative principles. This cartoon was in the then new style of drawing introduced by 'Ape', the best of the cartoonists in *Vanity Fair* for over 40 years.

THE LION'S SHARE.
" Gare à qui la touche ! "

☞ The acquisition of the Suez Canal Shares was accepted by the country as securing the safety of " The Key to India."—1876.

John Tenniel
Punch
26 February 1876
Disraeli as Prime Minister gained control of the Suez Canal on behalf of the British Government. Under the noses of the French, Disraeli was able to purchase a controlling interest in the canal from the ruler of Egypt, Khedive Ismail who was in desperate need of funds having just become bankrupt. The canal gave the quickest and calmest route to the jewel in Britain's imperial crown, India – thus the key.

John Tenniel
Punch
3 August 1878
Lord Salisbury as Foreign
Secretary with Disraeli now
Earl of Beaconsfield shared the
diplomatic triumph of a
settlement in relation to Turkey
at the Congress of Berlin. They
were both made Knights of the
Garter in recognition of their
achievement. The distinctions
of Marquis and Earl are shown
in their head gear.

Carlo Pellegrini 'Ape'
Vanity Fair
9 March 1872
William Henry Smith
This cartoon described W H
Smith as Statesman No 107 and
added the title 'Newspapers'.
Smith created the eponymous
retail chain, and had the
distinction of being the first
member of a Cabinet who came
from commerce.

CHAPTER 4

CONSERVATIVES AND LIBERAL UNIONISTS

1880—1902

As Prime Minister, Benjamin Disraeli led the Conservatives into the General Election of 1880. Personally exhausted, and as a member of the House of Lords, he did no campaigning. Gladstone's high moral tone brought him to government, with a majority of Liberals and Irish MPs.

The Marquis of Salisbury, originally a strong critic of Disraeli both as a person and as a policy maker, left the Cabinet as an opponent of the Reform Act of 1867, but rejoined in 1874. On Disraeli's death in 1881 he became the leader of the Conservative Party. His bulk and the full beard concealing his face gave physical expression to the immobility of his political views and actions. Cartoonists like Harry Furniss and Sir John Tenniel in *Punch* could make little of him. He was the first Prime Minister to be cartooned in a (small circulation) newspaper, by Francis Carruthers Gould.

Stafford Northcote had become party Leader in the House of Commons when Disraeli went to the Lords. He received a barrage of criticism from the so called Fourth Party – a grand name for four MPs including Balfour and Lord Randolph Churchill whose criticisms of Northcote coincided. They believed in continued aggressive opposition to Gladstone's Government and to Northcote. Northcote was eventually displaced.

The electorate was increased by 80% – six million new voters – by the Third Reform Act of 1884. Like the previous reform this had no immediate impact on the fortunes of the Conservative Party. The Liberal government was defeated on its budget in June 1885 and was followed by a minority Conservative Government under Salisbury. The General Election of December 1885, however, brought the return of Gladstone. His Liberal Party was supported by Irish MPs demanding Home Rule for Ireland, of which Gladstone was now a determined proponent. This, rather than the results of the 1884 Reform Act, was responsible for the largely Conservative Governments which followed. In March of 1886 Joseph Chamberlain, who had risen in power and influence in the Liberal Party as a middle class social reformer, resigned over Home Rule. He joined in defeating Gladstone's Home Rule Bill in 1886 with Conservatives who believed that neither British nor Imperial interests were served by Home Rule. In the following General Election Chamberlain and his followers were largely unopposed by Conservatives. Three hundred and sixteen Conservatives and 79 Liberal Unionists heavily outweighed 190 Liberals and 85 Irish 'Home Rulers', followers of Parnell. Gladstone's insistence on Home Rule kept the Liberal Unionists separate from his party.

Randolph Churchill, who had served as Secretary of State for India in Salisbury's minority Government, reached his peak as Chancellor of the Exchequer. Like many politicians before and after, he threatened resignation in order to pursue his own policy and was surprised to find that Salisbury let him go. Goschen took over, a Liberal Unionist remembered only because he was Churchill's successor.

CONSERVATIVES AND LIBERAL UNIONISTS · 1880–1902 CHAPTER 4

Conservative policy in Ireland, described as either coercion or oppression, was carried through by Arthur Balfour – known as Bloody Balfour as a result. Balfour received the approval that was natural within the Conservative Party for anyone carrying through a tough policy – in this case against an increasingly violent segment of the Irish population. Balfour, Salisbury's nephew and also effective deputy, became Leader of the House of Commons and heir apparent at the age of 43 in 1891.

The General Election of June 1890 brought yet another Gladstone minority government, Liberals depending on Irish Nationalists. Gladstone got his final Home Rule Bill through the House of Commons but it lost heavily in the Lords. Joseph Chamberlain accepted the logical consequence of this now lengthy split from the Liberals by agreeing that Liberal Unionists would join a future 'Unionist' Government – and indeed they had four Cabinet posts in the Conservative Government of 1895. This was the biggest of a succession of Liberal absorptions by Conservative governments.

Chamberlain chose to become Colonial Secretary instead of Chancellor of the Exchequer, thus surrendering the influence he might have had to bring about the social policies which he had advocated earlier. His was the major British political influence which brought about the Boer War of 1899, through which Britain forced the creation of South Africa as part of the Empire. The British electorate showed in the General Election of 1900 (the Khaki Election) that it was prepared to reward military success rather than being dismayed by some of the ways in which success had been achieved (the senior Liberal Campbell Bannerman had used the phrase 'methods of barbarism'). The Conservatives, now described as Conservatives and Unionists or just as Unionists, won the September 1900 election massively – over one third of constituencies were not contested. 402 Unionists faced 144 Liberals, 82 Irish Nationalists – and two Labour MPs. Salisbury finally surrendered the Foreign Office – to another Marquis – Lansdowne.

In July 1902 Salisbury passed on the Premiership to Arthur Balfour. He passed on also Joseph Chamberlain. Chamberlain knew that he could not be Prime Minister, but he determined that it should be his policy on Tariffs which would determine Unionist policy. A period which had seen the sundering of the Liberal Party over Home Rule was now about to see the same man precipitate great problems in the Unionist Party.

John Tenniel
Punch
March 1884
Lord Randolph Churchill
competes with Sir Stafford
Northcote for the leadership.
Whether *Punch*, and Tenniel,
actually saw Lord Randolph as
a clown is not known.

"MISSED AGAIN!"

Lord R. (as Clown).—"Out o' the way, Old 'Un! and let Me come!"

J Gordon Thomson
Fun
4 July 1888
Salisbury now Prime Minister is
linked with Hartington, joint
leader of the Liberal Unionists.
Their increasing cooperation
ensured the survival of the
Conservative government
despite Gladstone's censure.

THE THREE-LEGGED RACE.

BALFOUR THE MARTYR; OR, THE NEW ST. PATRICK.

ERIN.—"AND IS IT ST. PAT DRIVING OUT THE VARMINT YE THINK YERSELF!—SURE, IT'S THE VARMINT ITSELF YE ARE INTOIRELY!"

J Gordon Thomson
Fun
14 March 1888
The Irish Maiden 'Erin' representing Home Rule criticises Arthur Balfour, Secretary of State for Ireland. Balfour's robes contain the label 'coercion', a description of his policy in Ireland, also represented by his policeman's helmet, rifle and bayonet.

THE FREEDOM OF THE PRESS

The *Shamrock* Newspaper
Strong Irish criticism of 'bloody Balfour' carrying both a knife and a means of snuffing out the torch representing the freedom of the press. Houses burn in the background.

53

John Tenniel
Punch
April 1887
The classically educated reader of *Punch* would recognise the allusion to Sisyphus, constantly trying to push a rock – in this case 'Irish Difficulty' – up a hill.

SALISBURY SISYPHUS.
" Unending task!"   *   *   *   *   *   *

Harry Furniss
Pen and Pencil in Parliament
June 1895
Salisbury is shown sweeping the Liberal Prime Minister Lord Rosebery out of government. Balfour and Joe Chamberlain (now willing to take office) are recognisable on the broom.

THE NEW BROOM. JUNE, 1895.

Francis Carruthers Gould
Westminster Gazette
31 January 1896
Joseph Chamberlain on joining the Conservative government of 1895 had chosen to be Colonial Secretary. In that office he had encouraged the 'Jameson Raid' through which the Boers in South Africa were attacked – unsuccessfully. Lord Salisbury looks mournfully at the consequences.

"SING A SONG OF JAMESON."

Sing a song of Jameson,
  Transvaal all awry,
Five hundred Chartered troopers
  All in a pie.

When the pie is opened,
  The music-halls will sing,
Isn't this a dainty dish
  To set before the King?

The Chartered Company's troopers who took part in Dr. Jameson's raid are released by the Boer Government and sent home to England.

Francis Carruthers Gould
Westminister Gazette
15 July 1895
Lord Salisbury is first shown
riding the Liberal Unionist
Chamberlain. But Liberals
suggested as in the second
cartoon that Chamberlain
showed in a speech in
Birmingham that he had
swallowed the Conservatives.

"WHICH SWALLOWED THE OTHER?"

Francis Carruthers Gould
Westminister Gazette
9 November 1900
Lord Salisbury included in his
government so many of his
relatives that it was called
'Hotel Cecil'. Lord Hugh Cecil,
dressed here as a Catholic
priest, was the one left out.

II.—ONE THAT WAS LEFT.

TO DOWNING ST
AND WHITEHALL

Lord Hugh Cecil
(Son)

Lord Selborne
(Son-in-law)

Mr. A. Balfour
(Nephew)

Mr. Gerald Balfour
(Nephew)

Lord Cranborne
(Son)

Lord Hugh (left behind) : Please, mayn't I go too?

J M Staniforth
News of the World
30 September 1900
A carter John Bull is shown refusing to swap horses as they enter the river 'South African Policy'. His existing team consists Balfour, Salisbury and Joe Chamberlain. Lord Rosebery, strangely in a peasant smock, is offering Liberal horses, Campbell Bannermann and Harcourt accompanied by Labouchere and Lloyd George.

NOT FOR J.B.

CARTER JOHN BULL: "Swop teams while crossing this 'ere stream, Rosebery? Not likely. What do 'ee take I for?"

Percy Fearon 'Poy'
Judy
30 July 1002
Lord Salisbury hands over the Premier's sword to his nephew Arthur Balfour. He might have succeeded without his uncle Robert's assistance. It is claimed that the phrase 'bob's your uncle' derives from their relationship.

A CECIL, HO!
One down—t'other come on.

CHAPTER 5

SPLITS AND COALITIONS

1902–1922

In July 1902, the Conservatives were about to encounter political turbulence and dissidence. Although references to 'The Unionist Party' were now as frequent as those to the Conservative Party, Joseph Chamberlain had never been a serious contender to be Prime Minister. In May 1903 he launched his Imperial Preference Campaign. He saw duty on all imports except those from the Empire as being the only way to create the finances necessary to pay for future welfare and for the navy – and to support the Empire. Balfour and most of the rest of the Cabinet were not convinced. Chamberlain resigned from the Cabinet in September 1903 and campaigned for his policy. Balfour played a clever political game by removing Free Traders from the Cabinet also. There must have been interesting family discussions before Austen, Chamberlain's son, accepted the post of Chancellor of the Exchequer. Over some months 14 Conservative Free Traders left for the Liberal Party, including Winston Churchill.

Conservative opinion remained split between Imperial Preference, Free Trade and Balfour's middle course, Retaliatory Tariffs. The only significant success of Balfour's Government was passing the Education Act in 1903, which provided a common financial system for all Secondary Education. Balfour submitted the resignation of his Government on 4 December 1905. In the subsequent General Election of January 1906 the Liberals secured a massive overall majority with 399 MPs, compared with 157 Unionists, 83 Irish and 29 Labour MPs.

Balfour had said during the General Election that "the great Unionist Party should still control whether in power or whether in opposition, the destinies of this great Empire." He did not have the MPs to put this proposition into effect, but Unionists in the House of Lords continued their history of rejecting Liberal Bills, for example on education, plural voting and licensing. It generally met Lloyd George's description of it as "Mr Balfour's Poodle". Their action in voting against Lloyd George's budget of 1909 saw their reverence for the constitution overcome by their revulsion at Lloyd George's proposals to tax land and levy an inheritance tax. Income tax was doubled from 3% to 6%! Balfour allowed Lansdowne and Halsbury in the Lords to lead their unelected colleagues to defy the Commons. In the resulting General Election of January 1910 the electorate did not give full support to the Liberal's outrage and the Unionists gained 100 seats. The Liberal Government survived, supported by Irish and Labour MPs. The Lords passed the budget in 1910, but the Government proposed a Parliament Bill, which would reduce power of the House of Lords. A further General Election in December 1910 produced the same stalemate in the Commons but, under threat of a huge creation of new peers, the 'last ditchers' in the Lords finally gave way. Balfour had survived the 'Balfour Must Go' campaign; but resigned in August 1911. Those who wanted stronger leadership supported either Walter Long or Austen Chamberlain as his successor; Andrew Bonar Law emerged instead. Lloyd George commented "the fools have landed on the right man by accident".

Bonar Law, incensed that the Government had not put the Home Rule bill before the electorate, proceeded to speak and act without compromise. "I can imagine no length of resistance to which Ulster can go in which I should not be ready to support them". Sir Edward Carson, leader of the Ulster Unionists, used even more violent language, including encouraging the Army not to obey political direction.

Conservatives were able to adopt their more familiar guise of patriotism when supporting the war in 1914, but Asquith did not bring them into Government until a crisis in May 1915. It was probably more a credit to their patriotism than to their thirst for office that they accepted relatively minor Ministerial jobs. In December 1916 Bonar Law helped Lloyd George to become Prime Minister as a dynamic replacement for Asquith. The Lloyd George Coalition was responsible for the Representation of the People Act in 1918 that gave the vote to all men over 21 and to nearly all women over 30. For the next 20 years women were more likely to vote Conservative than either Labour or Liberal.

Lloyd George and his partners gained electoral success from winning the War in the 'Coupon' General Election of December 1918. Liberals remained split between two factions; only 30 Asquithians were returned compared to 130 Lloyd George Liberals. But Conservatives elected as Coalitionists were triumphant – 380 of them. So there was no doubt about whose policies would be predominant. Baldwin subsequently characterised many of them as "a lot of hard faced men who looked as if they had done very well out of the war".

Bonar Law resigned as leader in March 1921 owing to ill health and Austen Chamberlain succeeded without a vote. Chamberlain's tenure was short, because Conservatives finally decided in their famous meeting at the Carlton Club in October 1922 that they wished to end the Coalition. They had become increasingly distrustful of Lloyd George. They disliked his foreign adventurism. There was also scandalised objection to the increasingly obvious sale of honours in which Lloyd George multiplied previous Conservative practice, without any benefit to them. Lloyd George immediately resigned and Bonar Law (temporarily restored to health) took over as the first Conservative Prime Minister for 17 years. His Cabinet was derided by Winston Churchill (still notionally a Liberal) as the Second Eleven because Austen Chamberlain and other senior Conservatives declined to join.

Stanley Baldwin, one of the second rank Ministers (President of the Board of Trade) was one of the most significant influences at the Carlton Club meeting. Of Lloyd George, who had been praised by Conservatives as 'a dynamic force', he said "a dynamic force is a very terrible thing; it may crush you, but it is not necessarily right". Baldwin was to demonstrate what an undynamic Prime Minister was like when he took over from Bonar Law as Prime Minister.

Asquith, who as Prime Minister had suffered the assaults of Bonar Law especially over Home Rule, is reputed to have said at Law's funeral service in Westminster Abbey that "it is fitting that we should have buried the unknown Prime Minister by the side of the Unknown Soldier". But Law had been an excellent leader in the kind of leadership that Conservatives desired.

G R Halkett
Pall Mall Gazette
13 February 1904
There were Conservatives opposed to Joe Chamberlain's imperial preference version of Tariff Reform, and Arthur Balfour's policy of neither supporting nor opposing it. This cartoon shows the Free Fooders Lord Hugh Cecil (stabbing a Balfour doll) and Winston Churchill in prams pushed by the Liberals Campbell Bannermann and John Morley. Churchill but not Cecil switched to the Liberals later.

THE FREE FOOD TWINS.

Nurse "C.-B." : "If you ask *me*, Miss Morley, my opinion is that you've got *your* young gentleman quite nice and comfortable in his pram. As for *my* young gentleman, he always was a bit restless, and when he's quite done smashing his doll, I expect he'll want to get out and walk by hisself."

[*Mr. Winston Churchill and Lord Hugh Cecil have both declared their intention to vote with the Liberal Party against the Government.*]

David Wilson
Daily Chronicle
Arthur Balfour is shown unable to move, tied by the alternative views on Tariff Reform. Note the hint of a monocle, representing Joe Chamberlain, on 'The Whole Hogger'.

PRINTED AND PUBLISHED BY "THE DAILY CHRONICLE," FLEET STREET, LONDON, E.C.

"We don't seem to fit."

Arthur Moreland
Political Postcard for Faulkner
(1905)
Arthur Balfour and Joseph
Chamberlain are
uncomfortably tied together.
Chamberlain saw the Unionist
Party as the only vehicle for
imperial preference. Balfour
wanted to retain Chamberlain
and his supporters in the
Unionist party, without
accepting his full policy.

ONE—IF NOT THE ONLY—WAY.

SYDNEY CARTON BALFOUR : "It is a far, far better thing that I do, than I have ever done ;
it is a far, far better rest that I go to, than I have ever known."

Percy Fearon 'Poy'
Manchester Evening Chronicle
5 December 1905
Arthur Balfour and his
Government resigned on
4 December 1905 without
calling a General Election.
He is portrayed as Charles
Dickens' character Sydney
Carton, who said as he
ascended the steps to the
guillotine "It is a far far better
thing that I do than I have
ever done".

A S Boyd
Daily Graphic
17 January 1906
There were huge Unionist
losses in the General Election
of January 1906. Balfour lost his
seat for Manchester East – thus
the happily seated Liberal.

13 March 1906
Arthur Balfour had a great
reputation as a debater in the
House of Commons. Sir Henry
Campbell Bannermann the new
Liberal Prime Minister gave a
furious reaction after 13 March
to Balfour's first speech on his
return to the Commons. He
referred to Balfour's light and
frivolous way of dealing with
great questions. "I say enough
of this foolery". Balfour's
posture in the cartoon was
characteristic of him, not
necessarily a reaction to the
giant Campbell Bannermann.

Mr. Balfour (on the Electoric Railway): "I shall find a seat presently."

"THE STRAPHANGER."

"O! it is excellent to have a giant's strength; but it is tyrannous to use it like a giant."—*Measure for Measure.*

64

"NOW YOU'VE ONLY COME TO CAUSE TROUBLE."

"It must be remembered that to provoke a rupture between the two Houses of Parliament has been the deliberate policy of the Liberal party ever since it came into power. That policy was known as 'filling the cup.' Violent measures were introduced of such a kind as almost to oblige the House of Lords to reject them."—*The Times.*

Arthur Moreland
Morning Leader
17 November 1909
The Unionist majority in the House of Lords had vetoed or drastically amended Bills passed by the Liberals in the Commons. On 10 November 1909 Lord Lansdowne, Unionist Leader in the Lords announced that Unionists would not pass the 1909 Finance Bill. Balfour had criticised Lloyd George's famous 'People's Budget' because it aimed to please the mass of voters at the expense of the rich.

THE OBSTACLE EXPERT.

Leo Cheney
Passing Show
Arthur Balfour sought to avoid making a statement of policy which would split his party over Tariff Reform. He skated round the issue, adopting neither free food nor full Tariff Reform.

G R Halkett

The Conservative and Unionist
December 1910
Conservative supporters of the
House of Lords have always
claimed that it is the last
defence against attacks on
essential liberties. This cartoon
is unusually dramatic for its
time as it gives encouragement
to this view.

THE GREEDY HAND!

Electors, keep a tight grip on the greedy hand.

E T Reed

Punch
7 June 1911
The cartoonist's representation
of Arthur Balfour shows him in
the bent and elongated form
identified by nearly all
cartoonists. The reason for the
choice of roles for others is not
always clear. F E Smith was
certainly witty but was
Touchstone not more a broad
comic? Andrew Bonar Law the
Scotsman, as Macbeth, is more
obvious.

His Majesty's Opposition.   From left to right :—Mr. Balfour (Ariel), Sir E. Carson (the O'Phelia), Mr. Wyndham
(Osric), Mr. G. Cave (Portia), Mr. F. E. Smith (Touchstone), Mr. Chaplin (Juliet), Mr. Bonar Law (Macbeth),
Mr. Austen Chamberla'n (Prince Hal).

A Forecast of the Shakspeare Costume Ball.

Sidney Strube
The Conservative and Unionist
December 1911
Arthur Balfour, tired and bored by his attempt to keep the Unionists together, resigned as leader on 8 November 1911. Only Stanley Baldwin of his successors received such a bland farewell from cartoonists.

JOHN BULL: "I thank you, Sir, for services which I shall never forget."

Francis Carruthers Gould
Westminster Gazette
4 September 1912
Arthur Balfour's successor Andrew Bonar Law was a committed opponent of Home Rule, implying support for the use of force by its antagonists in Ulster. Sir Edward Carson was even more vehemently aggressive.

DANGEROUS LEADING

Ruby Lind
Suffragette
5 September 1913
Suffragettes were being imprisoned and force fed, but no action was taken against the speeches of Bonar Law and Sir Edward Carson which seemed an incitement to violence by Ulster Unionists. Ruby Lind, the wife of Will Dyson drew this in a very similar style to him.

THE NEW CHIVALRY.

ASQUITH (Guardian of Law and Order) to Mr. Bonar Law and Sir Edward Carson:
"As for you, sirs! Your sex protects you."

Francis Carruthers Gould
Westminster Gazette
28 May 1915
Prime Minister Herbert Asquith conducted the first nine months of the First World War through his Liberal government, but with Unionists offering 'patriotic support'. Criticisms by Lord Northcliffe, and failures in the Dardanelles forced Asquith to create a Coalition government. Asquith and Bonar Law are supported here by Unionists Carson, Balfour, Austen Chamberlain and Lansdowne.

THE COMPOSITE ORDER.

Carson-Kitchener-Crewe-Balfour-Grey-Lloyd George-Austen C.-McKenna-Lansdowne.
CABINET ARCHITECTURE.

IMMEDIATE ACTION.

ASQUITH: "Now, Bonar, this is one of those things that 'brooks no delay.'

Frank Holland
Reynolds Newspaper
3 December 1916
Dissatisfaction with Asquith's war leadership continued; newspapers and some politicians wanted a more active (and effective) war effort. The underlying reference in the text is to the fact that the country had been told in 1911 that reform of the House of Lords 'Brooks no delay'. Bonar Law helped force Asquith out on 6 December.

AN IDEAL REALISED.

Sidney Strube
Daily Express
1 May 1919
Austen Chamberlain, Lloyd George's Chancellor of the Exchequer, is saluted by his father's ghost as he introduces some items of Imperial Preference in his Budget address in the House of Commons.

David Low
Star
8 December 1919
Low's first great allegorical creation was the two-headed donkey that characterised Lloyd George's coalition government between 1918 and 1922. The donkey was according to Low like the coalition itself 'without pride of ancestry or hope of posterity'. Michael Foot believed that the constant appearance of the donkey in the *Star* undermined Lloyd George's coalition possibly more than any other single factor.

EXPLANATION.

Percy Fearon 'Poy'
Daily Mail
4 March 1920
Disputes between Liberals and Unionists within Lloyd George's coalition caused Bonar Law and Lloyd George to consider fusion into a single party. This cartoon shows the 'Wee Frees' (Asquith's independent Liberals) as the first obstacle; in fact it was the Conservatives who ended the proposal.

He will never get over

CHAPTER 6

THE NATURAL PARTY OF GOVERNMENT

1923–1945

When Bonar Law resigned after only seven months as Prime Minister in May 1923 the Foreign Secretary Lord Curzon seemed the natural successor to many, especially to himself. But Stanley Baldwin, derided by Curzon as "a man of the utmost insignificance" took over. He was more acceptable to his colleagues, but Curzon's membership of the Lords was the main factor in King George V's choice. (There was no mechanism for a vote by MPs.)

Baldwin was described by David Lloyd George as "the most formidable antagonist whom I ever encountered", and by Winston Churchill in his memoirs after 1945 as "the greatest party manager the Conservatives ever had". However, he lost his first General Election in 1923 over tariffs. In October 1924, Baldwin dropped Protection, the Liberal vote collapsed again and the Conservatives regained power. Churchill became Chancellor of the Exchequer, although he was not even formally a Conservative – he had been elected as a Constitutionalist MP for Epping with Conservative support. His five years as Chancellor are remembered primarily for his one major decision, to return to the Gold Standard in 1925. Unfortunately all but one of the experts he consulted agreed on the return. The exception was John Maynard Keynes, but his views did not have the authority necessary to overcome what J K Galbraith later called "conventional wisdom".

The General Strike of 1926 was called in support of the miners, but collapsed after ten days. The Lord Chancellor, Lord Birkenhead, remarked that it would be possible to say without exaggeration about the miners' leaders that "they were the stupidest men in England if we had not had frequent occasion to meet the owners".

Baldwin gained part of his subsequent reputation as a moderate by toning down the legislative consequences of the strike in the Trades Disputes Act of 1927. He lost the 1929 General Election, campaigning under the slogan "Safety First". While subsequently decried, this was an entirely appropriate slogan for a Conservative, particularly in tune with Baldwin's own, reassuring, slightly bucolic, pipe smoking image, often used by cartoonists. Baldwin had now lost two out of three General Elections as Prime Minister. Critical comments were made about his leadership. He overcame them firstly by winning a famous by-election at St. George's Westminster in January 1931, and then by the speech in which he addressed head on his most powerful critics, Lord Rothermere and Lord Beaverbrook, owners of the *Daily Mail* and *Daily Express*. August 1931 saw the great political crisis as the Labour Cabinet could not agree on economies in public spending. The Labour Prime Minister, Ramsay MacDonald, accepted the King's request that he should form a National Government with Conservatives and Liberals.

Baldwin was effectively MacDonald's deputy for the next four years. He was happy to support the concept of a National Government by letting MacDonald remain as Prime Minister. The National Government was set up purely to deal with the immediate financial crisis, but quickly fought a General Election in search of a 'Doctor's Mandate', to do anything necessary in order to restore the country's economy. The Government's supporters were returned in huge numbers, 473 of them Conservatives against 59 Labour. There were 13 National Labour supporters of MacDonald.

While Herbert Samuel and his Free Trade Liberals left the Government in September 1932, Sir John Simon and the National Liberals stayed. Simon's reward for his continued engagement was to be Foreign Secretary, Home Secretary and finally Chancellor of the Exchequer.

Baldwin, who became more soporific and who required frequent expeditions to Aix-les-Bains in the south of France to restore his health, replaced MacDonald as Prime Minister in June 1935, in time to see the India bill passed in July, despite 100 Conservative die-hard opponents led by Churchill.

There were large-scale protests from the unemployed. While there was a gradual improvement in the standard of living of those in work, the millions out of work (more, relatively, than in the 1980s) were subjected to a miserable level of benefit. Also, the level of intrusion into their financial circumstances – the means test – was a constant reminder of their misfortunes. This Government behaved as a Conservative Government was expected to – it believed that some how or other capitalism would gradually put things to rights. There were no measures comparable to those of Roosevelt's 'New Deal' in the United States. The General Election of 1935, although giving an improvement of 94 seats for Labour, produced no mass revulsion about unemployment.

German nationalism under Hitler suggested a need for rearmament, but Baldwin said before the General Election of 1935: "I give you my word there will be no great armaments", and was accused (unfairly) in Churchill's memoirs after 1945 of "putting Party before Country". He was faced by a Labour opposition that was opposed to rearmament for most of the time before 1939.

Anthony Eden as Foreign Secretary described the policy then as 'appeasement' in relation to Nazi Germany, a term which was subsequently used as a term of abuse. Eden resigned over Neville Chamberlain's interference over policy in Italy and not over appeasement as is widely believed. The vigorous opponents – very few – revolved around Winston Churchill. Churchill's opposition reached its peak with the Munich Crisis of September 1938, when Neville Chamberlain, now Prime Minister, returned to this country repeating Disraeli's claim about 'Peace in our Time'. Yet Churchill was distrusted by most Conservatives, accused of being an inveterate seeker after wars, and guilty of misjudgements.

Baldwin retired after managing the abdication of Edward VIII. He was followed in May 1937 by Neville Chamberlain who had, by Conservative standards, been a good Minister of Health and Chancellor of the Exchequer, but in foreign affairs his mixture of inexperience, ignorance and arrogance brought disaster. He became a political example of a principle enunciated by a management theorist in the 1960s, that every manager "is promoted to the level of his incompetence". Chamberlain moved step by step with the French in tow in the German dismemberment of Czechoslovakia, referring to "a quarrel in a far away country between people of whom we know nothing". The Munich 'Settlement' was a disgrace, not least, because the Czechs, having a significant army and fortifications and with the support of Britain, France and the Soviet Union, could have possibly withstood a German attack.

The failure of his foreign policy was manifest when he had to declare that a state of war existed with Germany, in September 1939. Labour refused to join a Coalition government under him and, as with Asquith, it took military crises to change that situation. Chamberlain's call to his friends to support him in the House of Commons in May 1940 failed when more than 100 Conservatives voted against him. Lord Halifax, with an appropriate combination of modesty and realism, agreed that Churchill, not he, should be Prime Minister. Churchill's focus on winning the war was quite appropriate to his talents, and had no unique connection with Conservative beliefs or policies. Churchill gave R A Butler a second ranking job as Minister of Education and was no doubt surprised when Butler produced a major Conservative reform with his 1944 Education Act. But whereas Labour responded with wholehearted concurrence to the famous Beveridge Report that proposed measures to deal with unemployment and sickness, Churchill and Conservatives were muted in their welcome.

Sidney Strube
Daily Express
19 October 1922
Conservative peers and MP's met at the Carlton Club to decide whether to go into another General Election in coalition with the then Prime Minister David Lloyd George. Their temporary leader Austen Chamberlain (Bonar Law was recovering from illness) was keen to keep the coalition together. When the vote went against him, Lloyd George was forced to resign as Prime Minister. In the cartoon, Chamberlain can be seen holding the hand of Lloyd George.

WILL HE GIVE HIS CONSENT?
There is keen speculation in political circles regarding the outcome of to-day's Carlton Club meeting.

A Tory Transformation.

BALDWIN—BEFORE AND AFTER TAKING THE PREMIERSHIP.

Frank Holland
Reynolds News
3 June 1923
Stanley Baldwin succeeded
Bonar Law, who would soon be
dead from throat cancer, as
Prime Minister on 22 May 1923.
Baldwin cultivated an image as
a countryman. Although
Chancellor of the Exchequer in
Bonar Law's government, he
had not previously been one of
the major figures – but many of
the others left with Austen
Chamberlain.

" DEAR, DEAR ! SURELY Mʳ ZINOVIEV HASN'T MISSED THE POST ! "

David Low
Evening Standard
27 May 1929
During the General Election of October 1924 the *Daily Mail* had published a (forged) letter from the chairman of the Comintern in the Soviet Union, Gregory Zinoviev, about the then Labour government's association with Russia. In the cartoon, Churchill, Baldwin, JCC Davidson (Conservative Central Office) and Joynson-Hicks wait in vain for a repeat. Low's cartoons occasionally as here featured a frightened cat.

Wyndham Robinson
The *Star*
9 May 1929
For the 1929 General Election Baldwin adopted the slogan 'Safety First'. This contrasted with the Liberal party, where Lloyd George's work creation scheme aimed at reducing unemployment.

AT THE CROSS-ROADS.

CAUTIOUS STANLEY : "These new Lloyd George roads frighten me ! "

John Reynolds
Morning Post
19 March 1931
In one of the most famous interwar by-elections press magnates Lords Beaverbrook and Rothermere put up their own candidate in St George's Westminster, in support of Empire Free Trade. He lost to the Conservative Alfred Duff Cooper by 6,000 votes.

Nazi Movement—Local Version

Will Dyson
Daily Herald
10 June 1933
Winston Churchill had resigned from the Conservative Shadow Cabinet over its proposals for a more independent India. The future opponent of Nazism is shown in a different role here.

Will Dyson
Daily Herald
20 February 1936
Stanley Baldwin had said in December 1935 that he could not give a full explanation of his policy over Abyssinia because "my lips are not yet unsealed. The stupidest thing I ever said", he confessed later. Dyson's comment relates to the Labour party's opposition to rearmament.

"*Follow me, brave lion.*"
"*But where to?*"
"*Sh! My eyes are sealed!*"

Jerry Doyle
The *Philadelphia Inquirer*
8 December 1936
An America cartoonist shows Baldwin dismissing King Edward VIII (David) during the Abdication Crisis.

In the Back-wash

" Racing at Henley is becoming too feminine."—Sporting Authority.

Con
Sunday Chronicle
14 September 1938
Neville Chamberlain's Munich Agreement was opposed by Churchill and his son-in-law, Duncan Sandys. Alfred Duff Cooper then the First Lord of the Admiralty was the only minister to resign over it. The implication in the cartoon that Anthony Eden led the opposition was inaccurate. Chamberlain observes from a distance.

A Machine For Three?

Mr. Chamberlain is said to be considering inviting the Opposition Leaders to join the Cabinet.

Middleton
Yorkshire Evening Post
18 February 1940
Neville Chamberlain's task would have been aided if he could have secured the support of the other main parties. They would not join in at the beginning of the war, nor would they do so in the final crisis of May 1940.

Leslie Illingworth
Daily Mail
7 May 1940
Neville Chamberlain claimed
that Hitler had lost the
initiative in the war and had, in
his words, "missed the bus".
This typically maladroit
statement preceded Hitler's
invasion of Norway. In the
cartoon, Ernie Bevin points at
the German leaders driving
past while Lloyd George and
the Liberal leader, Sir
Archibald Sinclair, shout at
Chamberlain to get a move on.
Churchill scowls on the lower
deck, while Sir John Simon,
Chancellor of the Exchequer, is
not surprisingly the conductor.

THE BUS

B T Ridgway
Daily Mail
8 May 1940
This caricature of Neville
Chamberlain appeared on the
day after the debate on the
Norway debacle which
ultimately led to his
resignation.

CHAMBERLAIN ANSWERS HIS CRITICS

"*This bomb should smash any ideas about a new Britain!*"

Philip Zec
Daily Mirror
17 March 1945
Winston Churchill's prestige as war leader was indeed to be the major Conservative weapon in the forthcoming General Election.

Wyndham Robinson
The *Star*
7 June 1945
Lord Beaverbrook, seen here, was influential in the Conservative campaign during the 1945 General Election. Huge crowds applauded Churchill where ever he went in the country but the Tory party was still discredited in most people's eyes for the high unemployment of the 1930s and for appeasing the dictators. As a result, Labour won a landslide victory.

George Butterworth
Daily Dispatch
7 June 1945
Winston Churchill in his famous broadcast of 4 June claimed a Labour government would have to set up some sort of Gestapo. Labour leader, Clement Attlee, sarcastically thanked him for showing electors the difference between the war leader and the party leader. In the cartoon, Ernie Bevin and Herbert Morrison, from behind the curtain, watch as the cartoonist portrays Attlee's response as a failure.

NO   CHANGE

David Low
Evening Standard
31 July 1945
This brilliant cartoon, drawn after the Conservatives' General Election defeat, epitomises Winston Churchill's career. As a war leader he had been exceptional but as a political one he failed both in 1945 and 1950 proving to be no electoral asset. Despite returning to office at the 1951 General Election, the Conservatives received fewer votes than the Labour Party.

TWO   CHURCHILLS

CHAPTER 7

CONSERVATISM REDEFINED ?

1945—1964

At the General Election of July 1945 Churchill launched broadsides against his recent Labour colleagues wholly reminiscent of his tirades against socialism in the 1920s. The Election produced the first Labour majority government, with 393 Labour MPs compared to 213 for the Conservatives and their allies. Churchill became a part-time and not very effective leader of the Opposition. The work on recreating the Conservative Party was done by Lord Woolton, a previously 'independent' Minister under Churchill, and by R A Butler as Chairman of the Conservative Research Department. Churchill finally returned to 10 Downing Street after the General Election of 1951, with a small but workable majority, although Labour had secured more votes than the Conservatives.

Churchill sought a peaceful environment on the domestic front while he pursued his ideas for creating a more peaceful world, proposing meetings at the 'Summit' with the leaders of the Soviet Union and United States. Through great will power, and an extraordinarily effective effort of concealment, his premiership survived a stroke in 1953. He was 79 in 1953, yet there were few public references to his age. Nor did cartoonists draw him differently, until Leslie Illingworth did so in 1954 (see Chapter 2).

The Conservative Industrial Charter in 1947 had implicitly accepted not to reverse the Labour Government's nationalisation of industry except for iron and steel. Nor were there reductions or significant change in social welfare arrangements, including the National Health Service (which the Tories had voted against in 1946). Churchill finally resigned in May 1955. Anthony Eden, the handsome and publicly charming Crown Prince since 1940, took over and called a General Election for 26 May 1955. The Conservative majority increased to 58. The Conservative share of the poll at 49.7% remains the largest for any party since the Second World War.

Eden appointed Harold Macmillan, now dangerously ambitious, first as Foreign Secretary, then as Chancellor of the Exchequer. Eden's great strength in foreign affairs was scarcely seen, since he declined the opportunity to participate in discussions that created the European Economic Community. His personal uncertainty was reflected in constant interference with his Ministers on domestic issues. The *Daily Telegraph* spoke of the absence of "the smack of firm government". In July 1956 Colonel Nasser, the Egyptian Prime Minister, nationalised the Suez Canal. Diplomatic efforts to ensure safe passage for shipping of all countries did not produce an answer that satisfied Eden and on 31 October the long delayed British military effort to retake the canal began. The Labour Party led opposition, while Eden and Macmillan misjudged the extent to which the United States would look the other way. The result was that after six days a ceasefire was called. Eden, fighting Hitler 20 years too late, collapsed physically and psychologically, and after two attempts to resume his role he resigned on 9 January 1957.

Even worse than the military and diplomatic failure involved was the gradual recognition that there had been collusion with France and Israel, who had also launched military attacks at the same time. Eden and his Foreign Secretary, Selwyn Lloyd, lied about this before, during and after the campaign. Eden left politics. Cartoonists had made little of him except his suited elegance and slightly exaggerated buck teeth.

Harold Macmillan, who had been derided as being first vigorously in favour of going in to Suez, then equally strongly insistent that we should leave, became Prime Minister. In the first of his many conjuring tricks he managed to persuade his colleagues that his certainty and strength (even when wrong) were preferable to the ambivalence of R A Butler. Macmillan, Prime Minister for nearly seven years, was a man of many layers of personality and levels of interpretation. He was the first Prime Minister to be satirised on stage (in *Beyond the Fringe*), whilst cartoonists also had plenty of fun with him (see Chapter 11). His dedication to full employment was given most visible demonstration when he accepted the resignation of his Chancellor and two other Treasury Ministers rather than accepting a small £50 million cut in Government spending, and referred to this as "little local difficulties". He encouraged an image of being unflappable, although in fact he was given to great attacks of nerves. His assertion in July 1957 that people had "never had it so good", became the description of the period.

The 1959 General Election was Macmillan's peak. Thereafter the economy bounced between boom and bust and Chancellors came and went. In 1960 he started the first British effort to join the existing six members of the European Economic Community. This was opposed by a significant portion of his party, a division that was to bedevil Conservative leaders for 40 years. At home, his efforts to sustain employment, if necessary by allowing some inflation, was balanced by an attempt to control inflation through increased productivity and a prices and incomes policy.

Macmillan's personal life was saddened by his wife's adultery, but he was hit by public scandals from a different direction, first by the discovery of John Vassall, a homosexual Admiralty official and spy and then by the much more damaging case of John Profumo, the Secretary of State for War, who lied over his relationship with Christine Keeler.

This supposedly unflappable man in fact took a panic decision to sack seven Cabinet Ministers in July 1962, including Lord Kilmuir who had claimed that "loyalty is the Tories' secret weapon". Jeremy Thorpe thrust in a dagger by inverting the injunction of Jesus that "greater love hath no man than to lay down his friends for his life". He resigned in October 1963 when he had prostate trouble. He set about managing the succession, favouring first Lord Hailsham and finally Lord Home, anyone to prevent R A Butler becoming Prime Minister. Home, having said he was not a candidate, backed into the limelight. He used the Act that had enabled Viscount Stansgate to become Tony Wedgwood-Benn to disclaim his own peerage. As far as cartoonists and political opponents were concerned Home could not disclaim the actuality of his aristocratic heritage. He sounded like an amateur in comparison with the tough Harold Wilson, and was an easy target for cartoonists with his skull-like face and thin lips.

For the General Election of October 1964 Labour campaigned on 13 wasted years, but won only a tiny majority.

David Low
Evening Standard
11 September 1946
After the shock of defeat in 1945 Harold Macmillan argued for a fusion of the Liberal and Conservative parties under a new name. David Low uses his image of Colonel Blimp to comment on the proposal. Low himself looks on from the left, RA Butler reads from a phone book. Macmillan asked Low for the original cartoon.

RECHRISTENING OF BLIMP

Jimmy Friell 'Gabriel'
Daily Worker
24 October 1951
There were ten Communist Party candidates for the October General Election. Gabriel makes a somewhat predictable assault.

Jimmy Friell 'Gabriel'
Daily Worker
6 October 1951
The Communist *Daily Worker*
not surprisingly took a vitriolic
approach towards the
Conservatives. Winston
Churchill, David Maxwell Fyffe
and Anthony Eden are on the
Conservative Planning
Committee. Oliver Lyttleton
and Harold Macmillan flank
Lord Woolton on Excess Profits.

Leslie Illingworth
Daily Mail
27 October 1951
Winston Churchill was restored as Prime Minister after the 1951 General Election victory. Sir John Tenniel's image of the sacking of Bismarck in his 19th century 'Dropping the Pilot' has often been used by cartoonists. Illingworth presents a clever reversal of the original.

David Low
Manchester Guardian
6 April 1955
Winston Churchill resigned as Prime Minister during a newspaper strike. Shoeless he tiptoes away accompanied by his wife Clementine.

SSH !

'Don't drop the pilot!'

Jimmy Friell 'Gabriel'
Reynolds News
16 September 1956
Another 'Dropping the Pilot' image. Eden is rejecting United Nations involvement in resolving the issues arising from Egypt's nationalisation of the Suez Canal.

Victor Weisz 'Vicky'
Daily Mirror
10 October 1957
The Conservative Party Conference followed Harold Macmillan's speech claiming that "most of our people have never it so good". The Government's problems are itemised by (from the left) Charles Hill, Lennox Boyd, David Eccles, Iain Macleod, Selwyn Lloyd and Duncan Sandys, Peter Thorneycroft and Lord Hailsham. On the right of Macmillan are John Boyd Carpenter, Henry Brooke, Reginald Maudling and Maxwell Fyffe.

THE BRIGHTON BUCKS
"Stop nagging, d-d-dear! I keep telling you that you've never had it so good!"

Leslie Illingworth
Daily Mail
8 January 1958
Macmillan departed for a
Commonwealth tour leaving
Butler in charge of the
Government's problems. The
largest box contains the
problems arising from the
resignation of all three of his
Treasury Ministers. Macmillan
referred to this as "little local
difficulties".

Frank Brown 'Eccles'
Daily Worker
28 September 1959
Macmillan looks worried in this
cartoon during the 1959
General Election. Eccles uses
Vicky's SuperMac title – but
misquotes Macmillan's 1957
speech.

WIND OF CHANGE

Glan Williams
News Chronicle
4 February 1960
Macmillan in his address to the South African Parliament said there was a wind of change blowing through the African continent. Without specifying apartheid he also referred to "some aspects of your policies" which prevented the British Government giving support to South Africa. The South African Prime Minister Hendrik Frensch Verwoerd is being blown over.

F Behrendt
Algemeen Handelsblad
1962
Macmillan is portrayed by this Dutch cartoonist as having "two souls in my breast" as he struggles to enter the European Economic Community while retaining ties to the Commonwealth.

Victor Weisz 'Vicky'
Evening Standard
17 July 1962
Macmillan sacked many ministers in what became known as the 'night of the long knives' on 13 July 1962. Vicky produced two versions of this cartoon on the same day presumably for different editions. The other version includes only the first seven names on the list thus excluding the names of the junior ministers that had also been sacked.

"But it really doesn't matter whom you put upon the list,
For they'd none of 'em be missed — they'd none of 'em be missed!"
—The Mikado

Michael Cummings
Daily Express
7 June 1963
John Profumo is seen lusting after Christine Keeler whilst the big fish in the guise of Harold Wilson awaits with glee the political repercussions for the Conservative Party over the Profumo affair. It is interesting to note how times have changed since 1963 that the cartoonist was instructed by his editor to cover mermaid Keeler's breasts with her flowing hair after the original drawing showed her breasts, in the cartoonist's words, "exposed in all their delightful glory".

'Smell? What smell?'

Leslie Illingworth
Daily Mail
12 June 1963
In its last days Macmillan's Government was beset by one scandal after another. The Ministers dining with him here are Gwilym Lloyd George, Edward Boyle, R A Butler, Iain Macleod, and Lords Home and Hailsham.

YOU CAN COME OUT NOW

Bill Papas
Guardian
19 October 1963
YOU CAN COME OUT NOW
Macmillan recovering in his hospital bed from prostrate surgery reveals Lord Home, his final candidate to succeed him as Prime Minister. Butler, Maudling and Hailsham look as if they need medical treatment too.

Frank Brown 'Eccles'
Morning Star
21 October 1963
The cartoonist mischievously reminds us that the new Prime Minister Lord Home, now simply Alec Douglas-Home, had been Neville Chamberlain's Parliamentary Private Secretary and had travelled with him to Germany to visit Hitler in September 1938.

The fourteenth Earl of Home,
He's got to number Ten,
He left his old umbrella there,
And he's got it back again.

Raymond Jackson 'JAK'
Evening Standard
17 October 1964
On 15 October, despite the Conservatives having been in office for 14 years, the Labour Party only gained an overall majority of four at the General Election. On the evening of the election it became known that Russian Premier, Nikita Khrushchev, had been deposed. Many commentators have since suggested that had the overthrow taken place a day earlier, the uncertainly deriving from it would have led to the Conservatives winning instead of Labour. In the cartoon, the now unemployed Khrushchev is seen joining the new Leader of the Opposition Sir Alec Douglas-Home for a shoot.

CHAPTER 8

CONSERVATIVES LOSE THEIR WAY

1965–1976

Sir Alec Douglas Home confessed – too late – that R A Butler would have been a better choice as Prime Minister. But he did facilitate the internal review that led to a decision that in future the leader would be directly elected by MPs. In July 1965 Ted Heath received 150 votes compared with Reginald Maudling's 133, and Enoch Powell's 13. These latter two withdrew and Heath became leader. After three Old Etonians he was the first lower middle class (at best) leader. Heath was thought likely to be more aggressive than Maudling in dealing with Wilson, but he was a wooden performer as a speaker in the Commons, on platforms and on television. He was faced within eight months with a General Election and produced a manifesto that was extraordinary for a Conservative. The surprise was not so much in any grand themes but in the fact that he made 131 promises for action. The electorate was unconvinced and Labour secured a large majority, on the lowest turnout since the war. Wilson's Government struggled, as so many had done since the war, with economic crises. The Conservatives were drawn together in January 1970 in a meeting at Selsdon Park Hotel, which would have been largely unremarkable if Harold Wilson had not hyped it as proposing a revolution in changing 25 years of social progress. The Conservative manifesto for the General Election in June 1970 opposed the wage and price controls that the Wilson Government in desperation had introduced, said there would be no privatisation of the nationalised industries and that another application would be made to join the European Economic Community if the terms appeared to be acceptable.

Enoch Powell had been one of the three Treasury Ministers who had resigned from Macmillan's government in 1962, had refused to join Home's Government in 1963, and had a reputation therefore for hard edged principle. He was in the Shadow Cabinet when he made a speech in April 1968 on immigration (see Chapter 12). This was a rumbling issue in all parties and there were legitimate concerns about the number of immigrants, particularly those visible because of the colour of their skin. Powell's inflammatory exchanges frightened immigrants but excited for a time considerable popular support. Heath sacked him.

Heath unexpectedly won the Election in June 1970 and his four years in Government divided roughly into two parts. He started by trying to carry out the policies on which he had been elected but, by 1972, he had turned the government engine into reverse, nationalising three companies to form the Upper Clyde Shipbuilders as well as Rolls Royce Aero Engines, and reintroducing prices and income controls as the economy worsened. Unlucky in facing a massive oil price increase and terrorism in Northern Ireland, he gave no sign of being in control of other events.

He did succeed in one area in which Macmillan and Wilson had both failed – he negotiated entry into Europe and signed the Treaty of Accession in January 1972. Conservatives were given a free vote and 39 voted against the European Communities Bill – but more Labour MPs than this voted in favour.

In January and February 1972 the miners called their first official strike since 1926 in opposition to the Government's policy of wage restraint, and gained most of what they demanded. But at the end of 1973 they struck again, leading to a three-day working week for the whole of industry. In February 1974 Heath called a General Election asking 'who governs Britain?'. The majority of the Electorate decided that they thought the Government should govern, ie manage the situation rather than call for a vote on an abstract principle. Heath unsuccessfully tried to do a deal with the 14 Liberal MPs, so Labour again formed a minority Government.

By October 1974 Labour had managed to placate the miners with a huge wage increase and in the General Election of October Labour secured a tiny overall majority of three. The Conservatives lost 20 seats. Heath remained largely oblivious to the dissatisfaction with him, no doubt because he had long ago lost contact with his backbenchers. He had lost three out of four General Elections, had gone back on manifesto promises and was personally unpopular. After October 1974 Heath had accepted the case for a leader submitting himself annually for re-election, without supposing it would immediately be applied to him. Keith Joseph was the first senior Cabinet Minister to put on a hair shirt and express his guilt over his actions in Government. When he ruled himself out of standing against Heath, Margaret Thatcher, who had been equally high spending as Secretary of State for Education decided to stand. William Whitelaw, the obvious candidate to replace Heath, refused to stand against him in the first ballot on the grounds of loyalty. Thatcher's friends cleverly manipulated the feelings of MPs to ensure that she actually secured 130 votes against Heath's 119. Those who had wanted Heath out but had voted for Thatcher only to create a vacancy, found themselves with a candidate whose bravery counted for more than Whitelaw's decent loyalty. Whitelaw was overwhelmed when he stood in the second ballot after Heath withdrew. This was recognised at the time as an extraordinary event – the first woman to be elected leader of a major political party in the UK. What was not recognised was that she would revolutionise British politics because of what she did, not simply because she was a woman.

Wally Fawkes 'Trog'
New Statesman
19 January 1965
Sir Winston Churchill died five days after this cartoon was published. The Babushka dolls give emphasis to Churchill's stature in comparison to his successors at No 10 Downing Street.

Michael Cummings
Sunday Express
10 January 1965
The cartoonist reminds us that Sir Alec Douglas Home as Prime Minister had admitted to using match sticks to help him try and understand economic policy. Having been defeated at the October 1964 General Election, Home remained leader of the party until his resignation in July 1965.

SUNDAY SPOTLIGHT . . . . . . by CUMMINGS

"She loves me . . . she loves me not . . ."

THE TORY TAPESTRY ···by GLAN WILLIAMS

Glan Williams
Sunday Citizen
25 July 1965
Whilst Leader of the Opposition, Sir Alec Douglas Home revised the rules of the Conservative Party to allow the party leader to be henceforth selected by a series of ballots of all Conservative MPs. The cartoonist prophetically shows how the Tory Party has a propensity to be disloyal to its leaders. To the right can be seen the leadership contenders, Reginald Maudling, Enoch Powell, Edward Heath and Christopher Soames.

Victor Weisz 'Vicky'
New Statesman
30 July 1965
The Tory leadership election was won by Edward Heath who defeated Reginald Maudling and Enoch Powell. Over the following six years, Sir Alec Douglas Home was notably loyal to Heath, comparing those who questioned his position with impatient gardeners who would keep digging up a tree to gauge its progress by examining its roots.

Edward McLachlan
Sunday Mirror
21 June 1970
Considering the pollsters thought Labour would win the 1970 General Election, Edward Heath surprisingly defeated Harold Wilson. In the cartoon, Reginald Maudling and Iain Macleod are train bearers with Douglas Home and Tony Barber as bridesmaids.

McLACHLAN'S VIEW

FOR BETTER . . . OR FOR WORSE

Arthur Horner
New Statesman
7 August 1970
Tony Barber, now Chancellor of the Exchequer, leads the Tory Government dancers Michael Noble, Margaret Thatcher, John Davies, Chris Chataway and Alec Douglas Home – with Prime Minister Edward Heath looking on.

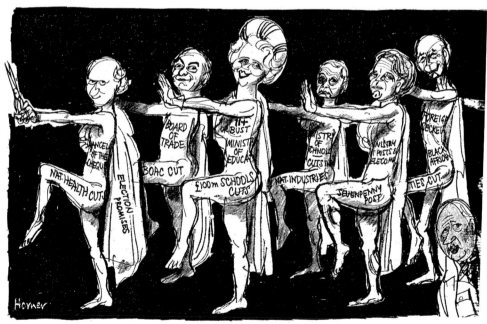

OKAY, CUTTER!
As the curtain goes up on the controversial new show at the Ranthouse, the cast come on in long white robes. The music plays, and they slowly and provocatively take off their robes and dance naked in the beam of projected credits.

"What was so marvellous about the rest of the British Commonwealth was that we could always leave it"

Michael Cummings
Daily Express
21 March 1971
Edward Heath and his Home Secretary, Reginald Maudling, survey the escalating problem in Ulster.

ALI BARBER

John Musgrave Wood
'Emmwood'
Daily Mail
20 March 1972
Chancellor of the Exchequer Tony Barber in his Budget of 21 March acted as all Conservative Chancellors would like to, by reducing a number of taxes. His budget was designed to return the Conservative party to power in an election expected in 1974 or 1975. However, this budget led to high inflation and wage demands from Public Sector workers and to a period that became known as 'The Barber Boom'.

Keith Waite
Daily Mirror
21 January 1974
Power cuts and the three day
week were amongst the
consequences of the miners'
strike early in 1974.   The
comment about Heath's
normally gleaming teeth
emerges from the trio of Barber,
Home and Willie Whitelaw.

"Still brushing them in the dark I notice"

Michael Cummings
Daily Express
8 February 1974
Edward Heath, accompanied
by Willie Whitelaw and Tony
Barber, prepares to battle in
the General Election against
Jeremy Thorpe (Liberal
leader), Enoch Powell (ex-
Conservative), Harold Wilson
(Labour leader) and the
miners' leaders Mike McGahey,
Jo Gormley and Lawrence Daly.

British-Crisis Handicap Event.

John Jensen
Sunday Telegraph
3 March 1974
The Conservatives found themselves with four fewer seats than the Labour party after the February General Election. Heath's attempts to draw the Liberal leader Jeremy Thorpe into a coalition proved unsuccessful.

Gerald Scarfe
Sunday Times
1 September 1974
Enoch Powell left the Conservative party because of his opposition to Edward Heath's intention to join the European Community. He became an Ulster Unionist representing the seat of Down South in Northern Ireland. The IRA was at the time carrying out a parcel bomb campaign on the British mainland.

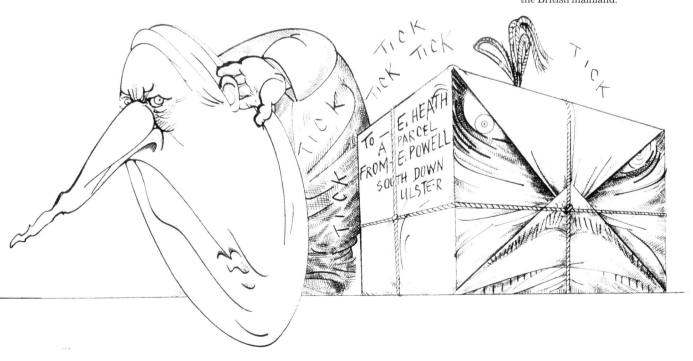

" I was going along quite happily when I suddenly found cars coming the other way . . ."

Nicholas Garland
Daily Telegraph
15 October 1974
Edward Heath lost his third
General Election as leader on
10 October 1974. His leadership
was now under threat.
Conservative Mps Edward Du
Cann, and Keith Joseph were
especially critical of him.
Interestingly the cartoon shows
Margaret Thatcher's minor role
as a critic of Heath's leadership.

Les Gibbard
The *Guardian*
12 February 1975
Margaret Thatcher was elected
Tory leader on 11 February and
is shown here as Joan of Arc.
This was one of the more
flattering cartoonists' images
over the years. She is followed
by James Prior, Home, Heath,
Whitelaw and Keith Joseph in
an assault on the Labour Prime
Minister Harold Wilson.

'Well, I trust those voices she hears are the voters!'

CHAPTER 9

NEW CONSERVATISM BEFORE NEW LABOUR

1976—1990

Thatcher was not elected to the leadership because she proposed an economic doctrine, 'Thatcherism'. She had been well behind in the polls until the 'winter of discontent' destroyed the Labour Government. The 1979 manifesto promised to cut income tax, proposed the right to buy council houses and made low-key references to the prospects of privatising nationalised industry. Yet the contempt for post-war consensus politics, which in fact drove her, was not fully revealed at the time. The Conservatives won three million more votes than in 1974, a durable working majority of 43, polling 44% to Labour's 37%.

In his first Budget as Chancellor of the Exchequer, Geoffrey Howe, made a reduction in direct income tax but doubled the rate on VAT. This was effectively redistribution from the poorer to the richer sections of society. Thatcher had been persuaded to use a quotation, misattributed to St. Francis, which included "where there is discord may we bring harmony". This was not in practice the tone of her time as Prime Minister. The immediate impact of her policies was 15 per cent inflation, a squeeze on commerce and industry and two million unemployed: a remarkable change from Macmillan and Heath. The moderates in her Cabinet, the 'Wets', murmured but did no more.

1982 saw yet another peak of three million unemployed as de-industrialisation continued. The impact of this was cushioned by welfare payments, and even more directly by the fact that Norman Tebbitt pushed through an Industrial Relations Bill that imposed more restraints on trades unions.

In April 1982 the fortunes of the previously unpopular Thatcher and her party were transformed when Argentina invaded the Falkland Islands, a British Overseas Territory. This aroused both the determination of Thatcher and her government to reverse the invasion, and patriotic fervour in Britain.

The result of the 1983 General Election at first sight seemed wholly due to the positive credits accrued by Thatcher through winning back the Falklands. Conservatives gained a further 80 seats and had a big majority. But the patriotic fervour, which on that theory pushed her back into power, is largely denied by votes cast – Conservatives achieved 42.4% of the poll, compared with 43.95% in 1979. Liberals and Social Democrats fed the majority – they obtained 25.4%, but few seats.

In April 1984 she acquired another major piece of fortune, when the egotistical miners leader Arthur Scargill led the miners into a strike without a vote to support it, at the wrong time of the year, i.e. March when coal was likely to be in less demand and after Peter Walker (the remaining wet in Cabinet) had made sure that coal stocks were high in case of such an eventuality. Even more than in 1974, this was a strike with an explicit political motivation – to be rid of the Thatcher Government. The Conservatives were not the only people to welcome its failure. Thatcher's good fortune and personal courage were shown in October 1984 when an IRA bomb placed in her Brighton hotel failed to kill her.

However, her luck began to run out. In January 1986 Michael Heseltine, the Defence Secretary, a massively successful Conference speaker who was both glamorous and ambitious, resigned. He became a potential candidate to stand against her. 1986 saw the final peak in unemployment at 3.4 million. Paying for the unemployed was an expensive part of the Conservative budget. They were able to do so while frequently lowering income tax only because of the impact of revenue from North Sea oil, council house sales, supplemented later by privatisation and eventually the economic boom of 1984 – 1986.

The June 1987 General Election again sustained the Conservative Government, despite a tiny fall in their vote by 0.2%. The SDP/Liberal Alliance stalled, and Labour marginally recovered.

Although Mrs Thatcher vehemently argued with her European colleagues for a rebate of our financial contribution when she became Prime Minister, the European Community was not otherwise on her hit list. Indeed in December 1985 she signed the Single European Act which involved the surrender of more British authority – and which she put through by a vote in Parliament, not through a referendum. In September 1988 Thatcher's increasing opposition to what was now called the European Community was expressed in a speech at Bruges in which she demanded that the boundaries of the State should be rolled back. In July 1989 she moved Geoffrey Howe out of the Foreign Office. In itself hurtful to him, the injury was amplified when her Press Secretary commented that the title of Deputy Prime Minister, which Howe now acquired, did not mean anything. In October Thatcher told the Conservative Conference that she intended "to go on and on", but questions were now increasingly being raised in the party about her judgement.

Unpopularity was compounded with the Community Charge, better known as Poll Tax. Tory MPs became increasingly concerned about the impact of this policy on the likelihood of retaining their seats. But it was Europe that brought about the end for Mrs Thatcher when her "No, No" reaction about Europe caused Geoffrey Howe to resign. On 13 November 1990 he spoke in Parliament with quiet dignity about the "tragic conflict of loyalties with which I myself have wrestled for perhaps too long". Heseltine stood against Mrs Thatcher in the now inevitable election in which she failed by four votes to get the required majority. She declared that she would fight a second time, but individual meetings with her Cabinet Ministers showed that the majority thought she would not win. She resigned on 21 November, the victim of MPs' self-interest, the ambition of Heseltine, her own increasing arrogance, the worm that turned. Her tears as she lost her job were unlikely to generate sympathy in the millions who had lost jobs and their livelihood under her government.

Thatcherism had transformed the economy, society and the basis of political conflict. Many Conservatives now wanted a quieter life.

John Jensen
Sunday Telegraph
6 May 1979
The Conservatives were victorious in the General Election on 3 May. The cartoonist poses the question, having become the first woman Prime Minister in British history, can Thatcher halt Britain's decline?

Michael Cummings
Daily Express
10 February 1980
Cabinet ministers opposed to the extremes of Thatcher's economic policies were referred to pejoratively by her supporters as 'wets' as Norman St. John Stevas, Willie Whitelaw, Lord Carrington and James Prior are portrayed here. In fact there was no risk at all of her being drowned by her opponents nor of Edward Heath sending his boat to rescue her.

"Here's another fine mess you've got us in!"

Nicholas Garland
Daily Telegraph
21 March 1980
Chancellor of the Exchequer Geoffrey Howe as Oliver Hardy faces problems in his 1980 Budget – some caused apparently by him (Stan Laurel) a year earlier.

John Jensen
Back on the House by Simon Hoggart
1982
William Whitelaw, defeated by Margaret Thatcher in 1975, became her Deputy Prime Minster. He was totally loyal to her and helped smooth down relations with her colleagues. In a tribute she must have written herself without appreciating its double meaning she said "every Prime Minister needs a Willie".

Nicholas Garland
Daily Telegraph
30 April 1980
Britain contributed about £1 billion more to EEC funds than it received. Thatcher at the EEC Summit meeting in April 1980 was obdurately determined to get 'our money' returned via a rebate. She was prepared to disrupt the whole meeting: a rebate was agreed.

Wally Fawkes 'Trog'
The *Observer*
16 November 1980
EEC conferences sometimes avoided time deadlines by stopping or setting back the clock. The cartoonist comments on the destructive effects of Thatcher's policies on British industry.

Keith Waite
Daily Mirror
9 October 1981
Heath was never reconciled to
Thatcher. Before the
Conservative Conference in
Blackpool he clashed explicitly
by calling for the abandonment
of 'dogmatic policies'. But there
was no real risk of the big shark
taking over.

Martyn Turner
The Irish Times
5 April 1982
This cartoon echoes a popular
and jingoistic music hall
anthem penned by G W Hunt in
the late 19th century which
expressed willingness to fight a
war. Thatcher faces the
Argentinean leader, General
Galtieri who had sent his
troops to occupy the Falkland
Islands, a British Territory.

Frank Brown 'Eccles'
Morning Star
9 June 1983
On the day of the 1983 General Election, the cartoonist inexplicably portrays the Tory cabinet as worried. In reality, with the Labour opposition in turmoil under the leadership of Michael Foot, the Conservatives were to romp to victory. In the cartoon, Thatcher leads, holding a reference to expensive cruise missiles, followed by Norman Tebbit, Geoffrey Howe, Willie Whitelaw, Michael Heseltine, Keith Joseph, Francis Pym and James Prior.

Peter Brookes
The Times
4 April 1984
The Government had prepared itself to meet a miners' strike by building up stocks of coal. The projected support of the miners by other unions refusing to move coal did not eventuate on a large scale.

"It will have no effect, you know."

114

"No, Michael, YOU'VE got it wrong—YOU Michael, ME Tarzan!"

Raymond Jackson 'JAK'
Evening Standard
23 December 1985
Michael Heseltine and Thatcher disagreed over whether a new helicopter for the armed services should be sourced in Europe or in the USA, as Thatcher wanted. Cartoonists had helped create an image of Heseltine as Tarzan – and this cartoonist correctly forecasts the victor in this dispute.

"As you're such a good back-seat driver, I've resigned as chauffeur — so you can change the wheel, yourself!"

Michael Cummings
Daily Express
29 October 1989
Chancellor of the Exchequer Nigel Lawson was increasingly in disagreement with Thatcher and her economics adviser Sir Alan Walters. When she refused to sack Walters, Lawson said that his position was becoming "untenable" and soon resigned.

Fritz Behrendt
Badische Neuste Nachrichten
4 November 1990
In the House of Commons on 30 October Thatcher vehemently rejected the possibility of a Federal Europe "No, no, no" she famously stated. This was the final straw for Geoffrey Howe whose subsequent resignation and speech led to a leadership contest.

Charles Griffin
Daily Mirror
14 November 1990
Thatcher on 12 November claimed that she was facing hostile bowling "but there would be no ducking bouncers". Howe's resignation speech the next day showed the consequence of not ducking.

Steve Bell
New Statesman
23 November 1990
Michael Heseltine followed Howe's speech with a decision to challenge Thatcher for the leadership. Denis Healey in 1978 had characterised a critical speech by Howe as like "being savaged by a dead sheep". The sheep reappears here in a different role. This cartoon is a pastiche of the painting by William Holman Hunt entitled 'The Scapegoat'.

Kevin Kallaugher 'KAL'
The *Economist*
27 November 1990
Michael Heseltine's challenge to Thatcher's leadership of the Conservative Party brought about her resignation. Many cartoons have used variants on the theme of Margaret Thatcher as the Iron Lady. This cartoonist dispatches her to the dustbin of history.

Les Gibbard
BBC TV 'On the Record'
November 1990
Michael Heseltine garnered
enough votes in the first
leadership election in
November to destroy Margaret
Thatcher. In the cartoon the
two tortoises – Douglas Hurd
and John Major – hurtle to
challenge him in the second
election.

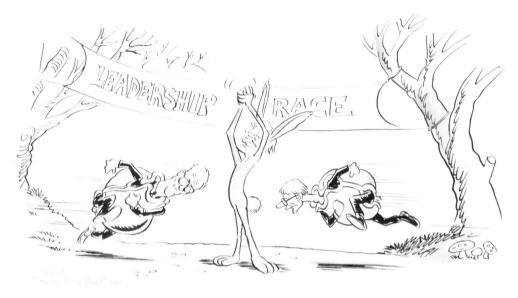

Michael Heath
The Independent
29 November 1990
The victor of the leadership
contest was Thatcher's
Chancellor of the Exche
quer, John Major. He was the
son of Tom Major-Ball, a retired
circus performer who was 65
when John Major was born.

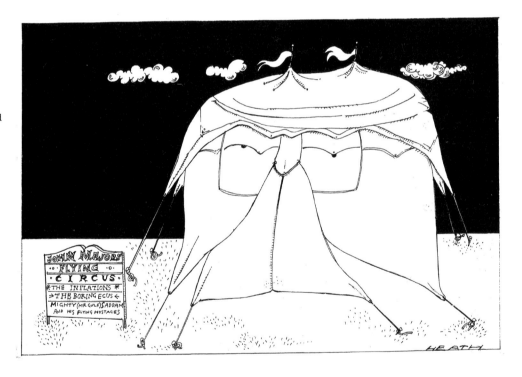

CHAPTER 10

UNEXPECTED SUCCESS TO PROLONGED FAILURE

1990–2008

John Major, Thatcher's choice to succeed her, was elected leader in preference to Michael Heseltine and Douglas Hurd. Comparisons with the vibrant leadership of Thatcher were made to the disadvantage of the obviously undynamic Major, and the polls for a long time suggested that Labour would win the General Election that Major postponed as long as possible to 9 April 1992. Major's decent common man image turned out to be more important than the grey anti-superman image presented by cartoonists. There was a small reduction in the Conservative vote, and Major's majority was only 24 compared with Mrs Thatcher's 102 in 1987. This meant he could expect to have problems with any rebels.

Major signed the Maastricht Treaty, expanding the role of the EEC, in December 1991. He had a battle to secure passage of the Treaty through the House of Commons, with 20 or more Tory rebels constantly voting against him. The Government's authority had been massively reduced when on 16 September 1992, 'Black Wednesday,' the expensive battle to stay in the Exchange Rate Mechanism, was lost. Neither Major nor the Chancellor Norman Lamont resigned. Major was stuck with a Chancellor whose credibility was totally blown, but whose policy he had shared. Lamont had claimed unemployment was a price worth paying, that he saw the green shoots of recovery when nobody else did, and then he quoted Edith Piaf "Je ne regrette rien". Major acquired another bitter enemy when eventually he sacked him.

Major suffered from his own phrase-making in October 1993 when he said the country needed to "return to core values". His PR men spun this as being "back to basics". Major meant it as decent Conservative personal values, but the spinning of his speech and the unfortunate conjunction of a series of financial and sexual misdemeanours by his MPs and a few Ministers enabled opponents to contrast what they described as 'sleaze' with his pronouncement. Major, the decent man, found himself defending individuals later proven to have lied to officials, to him and to the courts. Economic mismanagement, European rebels and sleaze all helped to create an image of a government tottering in decline. Major decided to try and face out his internal critics by resigning the leadership in July 1995 and fighting against John Redwood, the one Cabinet critic who had the courage the stand against him. Major won by 212 votes to 89, not a comfortable result for a sitting Prime Minister.

When the General Election of May 1997 arrived Major was faced with Tony Blair, young, attractive, not credibly described even by Conservatives as a socialist. Labour rose from 34.4% to 43.2% and the Conservatives crashed from 41.9 to 30.7%. As always, the subsequent huge Labour majority was a reflection of the 'first past the post' system. Major resigned immediately and went off to watch cricket at the Oval.

Major's problem for many Conservatives was that he was not Margaret Thatcher. Margaret Thatcher's problem was that he was not Margaret Thatcher. Just like Heath she did not accept that her dismissal had been legitimate. The difference was that she retained a core of support, which echoed her increasingly less private criticisms of Major. Now she engaged publicly in supporting a particular candidate, the youthful William Hague, to take the leadership. Europe had become a constant imbroglio for the Conservative party.

Conservative MPs rejected the obviously credible Kenneth Clarke as leader because he was pro-Europe. Hague raised Conservative morale internally both in the House of Commons, where he was brilliant at Prime Minster's Question Time, and in the country. But the Conservative vote increased by only one per cent at the 2001 General Election and Hague resigned immediately. In the subsequent leadership election, now shared between MPs and constituency members, Kenneth Clarke was again beaten, this time by another but older bald man, Iain Duncan Smith. It was the European stomach ache again. Smith, largely unknown to the public, was a rebel over the Maastricht Treaty. Unlike Hague he was a poor speaker on platform and TV, and his attempt to convert a weakness into strength at the October 2002 Conference – "never underestimate the determination of a quiet man" – was received with mockery. He resigned when he lost a vote of confidence in the parliamentary party in October 2003.

The Conservative Party had tried youth with Hague in 1997 and inexperience with Duncan Smith in 2001, and now turned to the experienced Michael Howard, anointed as leader without an election. Howard had been an unpopular Conservative Minister, but had worked diligently to support whoever was Leader since 1997. His apparent return from the wilderness was a boon for cartoonists. Conservative grassroots had no problem identifying with a man who, as Home Secretary, had said "prison works". The Conservatives could not capitalise on the unpopularity of the Iraq War in the 2005 General Election since the party supported it. Their vote went up only to 32.4%. Howard, like Major and Hague, resigned immediately. Conservatives indulged in public democracy as candidates, including Kenneth Clarke, travelled the country making speeches at 'hustings'. The Conservatives might have chosen the apparent favourite, David Davis, the product of a one-parent family from a housing estate in London. Instead they chose David Cameron who was young, educated at Eton and Oxford with four and a half years in the Commons and no significant frontbench experience. Cameron's success was at least in part created by his final hustings speech at the Special Conference, where he spoke without notes, moving easily around the platform instead of being fixed to a lectern. Cameron's theme was that the party needed to cut itself away from a large part of its past, ie those parts which still could be used to attack them. He was anti-European and therefore acceptable to the majority of the party but presented a cleaner young image with apparent eagerness to adopt new policies.

Michael Heath
The Independent
30 November 1990
John Major adopted a different Prime Ministerial style to that of Mrs. Thatcher, which was essentially far more collegial. Major was a great user of his cabinet team and encouraged discussion of government policy in order to gain opinions and feedback. Under Major, the cabinet had greater influence over the direction of policy than had been the case with previous Conservative administrations. Major's first Cabinet did not include any women.

Steve Bell
Guardian
7 March 1991
The cartoonist hits Major three times in one cartoon. As oil wells from the war against Iraq in Kuwait burn Major appears in Bell's defining characterisation for him as a nerdy Superman. He has also caught the sometimes strange wording of Major's speeches and his duck like upper lip. (Russian President Mikhail Gorbachev has been overcome.)

'WHO SAYS WE DON'T HAVE A WOMAN IN THE CABINET?'

"Rest assured, Madam, the Forces of Inflation won't advance while we have men to throw at them!"

Les Gibbard
Guardian
17 May 1991
Chancellor Norman Lamont's view of unemployment was that it was a price worth paying. He and Major preside over a modern version of the First World War battle of the Somme.

"Norman — are you sure this fable has a happy ending?"

Dave Gaskill
Today
2 April 1992
The Fable of the Tortoise and the Hare reappears as Major and Lamont are knocked aside by Neil Kinnock and John Smith as they approach the General Election. However, Major had the happy ending when he, to every pollsters' surprise, won an overall majority of 21.

Steve Bell
Guardian
19 January 1995
A successful Conservative election poster in 1979 had claimed that Labour wasn't working, with a long queue of unemployed people. Chancellor of the Exchequer Kenneth Clarke is faced with this historical image.

Chris Riddell
The *Observer*
2 July 1995
MP's had long congratulated themselves on being the most sophisticated electorate – which in practice meant lying about who they would vote for in leadership elections. John Major resigned as leader and then stood again in order to re-establish commitment to his leadership. John Redwood, nicknamed the Vulcan because of similarities between him and Star Trek's Mr Spock, resigned from the Cabinet in order to stand against him. Heseltine remained loyal.

Martin Rowson
New Statesman
23 May 1997
John Major resigned as Tory Leader after Labour's landslide victory in the General Election of 1997. At the age of 36, William Hague was chosen by the Conservatives as their new leader. Because of his youth. Hague was regularly portrayed as a schoolboy. In this cartoon he is portrayed in a nappy, an obvious visual euphemism for inexperience and immaturiy.

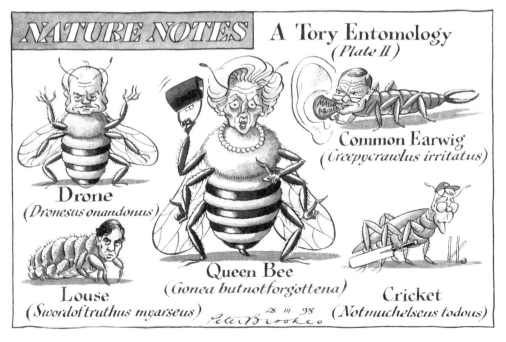

Peter Brookes
The Times
28 March 1998
The cartoonist presents some Conservatives as insects in his regular *Nature Notes* series. William Hague the leader is a drone, Thatcher swings a handbag, and Jeffrey Archer is identified as prospective candidate for Mayor of London. Jonathan Aitken, who had proclaimed that he held "the sword of truth", had lied in his libel trial. John Major was frequently observed at cricket matches.

Dave Brown
The *Independent*
9 October 2001
William Hague emphasised scares about Europe before the 2001 General Election. The cartoonist finds more scary Conservatives – Ann Widdecombe, Michael Portillo, William Hague and a mummified Thatcher.

Paul Thomas
Daily Express
30 October 2003
The party chose Iain Duncan Smith to replace William Hague as leader after the 2001 General Election. He had told the Tory Conference in 2002 not to underestimate the determination of a quiet man (himself) but he lost the confidence of his MPs and resigned.

Andy Davey
The *Independent*
6 November 2003
Anne Widdecombe declared
about Michael Howard in the
1997 leadership election that
he had "something of the
night about him". His re-
emergence as leader was one
the more extraordinary events
of 2003. Clarke and
Widdecombe have failed to
put a stake through his heart.
Thatcher features as a bat.

Chris Riddell
The *Observer*
6 March 2005
Michael Howard as leader did
his best to worry the electorate
about the consequences of a
third Labour election victory,
but cartoonists continued to
draw him negatively as Count
Dracula primarily because of
his Rumanian origins and Ann
Widdecombe's earlier
comments.

Peter Schrank
The *Independent on Sunday*
16 October 2005
David Cameron leaps from a
disintegrating Tory structure
towards the leadership. The
Tory torch was still the party
symbol.

Morten Morland
The Times
24 October 2005
One of David Cameron's early
attempts to reposition the
party involved more apparently
sympathetic recognition of
social problems, particularly
amongst youth. The cartoonist
points out the incongruities
involved.

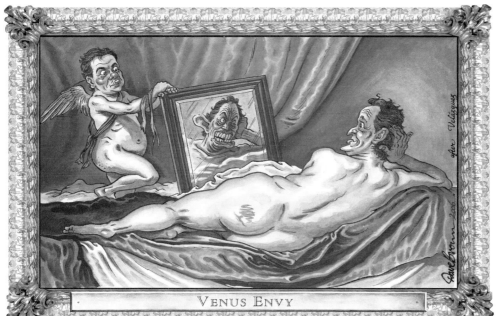

VENUS ENVY

Dave Brown
The *Independent*
2006
The Conservatives did away
with their old torch logo in
order to replace it with a tree.
This was to emphasise the
party's new green credentials.
Cartoonists have often used
paintings by well known artists
as the basis for a cartoon.
Brown has developed a regular
series called 'Rogues Gallery'.
Here the original painting by
Diego Velazquez is used to
show Cameron bidding to
occupy New Labour territory
seeing himself as Tony Blair.
The mirror is held by the
shadow Chancellor George
Osborne.

Peter Brookes
The Times
4 October 2007
David Cameron during the final
hustings in the leadership
campaign in 2005 had spoken
without a script. He repeated
this style at the Conservative
conference at a time when
Labour looked likely to call –
and win – a General Election.

Martin Rowson
The Guardian
5 May 2008
Boris Johnson became the
Conservatives greatest
electoral success since John
Major's surprise victory in the
1992 General Election when he
defeated Ken Livingstone for
the post of Mayor of London.
Johnson had initially been
dismissed as the Bertie Wooster
of British politics but won
42.48% of the vote compared to
Ken Livingstone's 36.38%.
Johnson reassured London that
he would do his best to
maintain his new serious image.
"I was elected as new Boris and
I will govern as new Boris, or
whatever the phrase is," he
joked in a pun on Tony Blair's
famous New Labour
declaration. David Cameron
also quickly hailed the result.

Christian Adams
Daily Telegraph
29 July 2008
Opinion polls showed a further
big drop in public confidence in
the Labour Government's
economic management. The
Conservatives now led Labour
by 19 points as the party best
able to deal with the situation,
compared with an 11-point
Labour lead in October the
previous year.

CHAPTER 11

SEEING THEM DIFFERENTLY

Carlo Pellegrni 'Ape'
Vanity Fair
1869

John Tenniel
Punch
9 November 1867

FAGIN'S POLITICAL SCHOOL.

J G Thomson
Fun
18 April 1874

THE BELLE OF THE SEASON.

Harry Furniss

DISRAELI ADDRESSING THE HOUSE

Carlo Pellegrni 'Ape'
Vanity Fair
2 July 1878

Fun
12 June 1878

ARTHUR BALFOUR – THE LAST INTELLECTUAL

After his defeat in the January 1906 General Election Balfour proclaimed that it was the duty of his colleagues to do their best "to see the great Unionist Party shall still control whether in power or whether in opposition the destinies of this great Empire". The Unionist majority in the House of Lords indeed did their best to fulfil this requirement over the Budget in 1909 and over House of Lords Reform in 1911. Balfour encouraged this opposition almost but not quite into the last ditch. A leader is supposed to be wiser than those he leads, and his response on these two issues was disastrously unwise. Balfour also may be seen to have carried out his 1906 statement in a different way. He spent 27 years as a Cabinet Minister, 12 spent initially on an apparently inevitable progress towards his three and a half years as Prime Minister, then 12 years under Asquith, Lloyd George and Baldwin. Although he was certainly encouraged and supported by his uncle and Prime Minister, the Marquis of Salisbury, his intellect, resolve and debating skills were of a quality to justify his elevation. But as Prime Minister he was beset by the issue – tariffs on imported goods – that had destroyed the Conservative Government almost 60 years earlier. He was determined not to repeat Peel's mistake of directing a policy that would break the party in two, and therefore chose an approach that satisfied neither Tariff Reformers nor Free Traders. His manoeuvres in trying to rebalance his Cabinet through resignations in 1903 aroused confusion at the time, and derision since. His attempt to wrong foot the Liberals by resigning the Government at a time when he thought the Liberals were in disarray in 1905 rebounded when he lost the subsequent General Election by a massive margin. His resignation as Leader in 1911 resulted from mutual dissatisfaction between himself and those he was supposed to lead.

He returned to government under those whom he had violently opposed, first Asquith in 1915 and then Lloyd George in 1916, under the different circumstances of War. It was during this time that Balfour's name became more indelibly highlighted in political British and World history, with his declaration as Foreign Secretary in 1917 on the fate he proposed for Palestine, giving land which was not his to give as "a national home for the Jewish people".

Balfour was the last intellectual Prime Minister. He published two books of philosophy. The first, *A Defence of Philosophic Doubt*, is entirely misleading as a representation of his career, since he was often very determined: for example his actions in Ireland gave him the designation 'Bloody Balfour'. Yet one of his aphorisms is very appropriate for a Conservative: "nothing matters very much and most things do not matter at all".

Cartoons on Balfour as an elongated lounger without a strong backbone, although probably correctly emphasising some aspect of his physique, are misleading as to his character. Cartoonists found it easy also to pick on his interest in playing golf (he was also an active tennis player).

Leslie Ward 'Spy'
Vanity Fair
24 September 1887

Arthur Balfour as Spy saw him. This cartoon hangs in the parlour at Number 3 St. James's Street.

Francis Carruthers Gould
Rhyme and Line
by Henry Lawson

" *What is right?   What is wrong?*
What are lies?   What is truth? "

Harry Furniss

left
Percy Fearon 'Poy'

right
E T Reed

Philip Sallon

Michael Cummings

... As if he is enjoying himself hugely!

Jimmy Friell 'Gabriel'
Daily Worker
18 October 1951

As Gabriel sees him.

David Low
Manchester Guardian
5 June 1953

Victor Weisz 'Vicky'
Evening Standard
28 January 1955

HAROLD MACMILLAN – THE ACTOR CONSERVATIVE

Harold Wilson's acute comment on him was "his role as a poseur was itself a pose". MP for an industrial Northern seat in 1924 he was at least partially educated in the realities of working lives very different from his own – Eton, Oxford, and marriage to a daughter of the Duke of Devonshire. In 1929 he lost first his seat, and then the fidelity of his wife Lady Dorothy to his friend, Robert Boothby, also a Conservative MP. In the 1930s he was a Conservative rebel, first over economic solutions to unemployment and then over Chamberlain's policies towards Italy and Germany.

During the war Churchill appointed him as resident Minister in North Africa, and later in Italy which led to a transformation in Macmillan's self belief and expression of it. Now MP for Bromley, he took a prominent position in the Conservative Opposition after 1945. Macmillan's success after 1951 in providing 300,000 houses was followed by a quick succession of senior but short-lived posts – Defence, Foreign Secretary and Chancellor of the Exchequer. Although his own role over Suez was disastrous since he misinterpreted the US response, he gained the benefit from sounding strong – he was preferred as Eden's successor to the sceptically ambiguous R A Butler. Macmillan had transformed himself from a boring speaker capable of emptying the House of Commons to an effective performer in the Commons and on television. Even then, however, his articulation sounded archaic.

As Prime Minister his pre-war experiences in Stockton substantially influenced him to give greater priority to full employment (including his relatives in Government) at the cost of some inflation. His claim that "most of our people have never had it so good" received more attention than the accompanying qualification that some people had not had it very good. He simulated indifference to the resignation of his complete Treasury team in 1958, referring to the event as "little local difficulties" as he departed on a tour of the Commonwealth. Africa was the stage and the content of his last great performance. He chose an address to the Parliament of Apartheid-era South Africa to say that there were "winds of change, which would transform the continent". He allowed Iain Macleod to accelerate decolonisation. He tried to take Britain into Europe, but met the entrenched opposition of an even greater actor, the French premier de Gaulle.

A quotation from Gilbert and Sullivan was in his office: "quiet, calm deliberation untangles every knot". In fact he was far from unflappable. He was frequently physically sick before major performances in the House of Commons. In July 1962 a move for Selwyn Lloyd from the Treasury ballooned into sacking one third of his Cabinet. In 1963, overcome by panic over prostate trouble, he resigned.

In a long retirement Macmillan had the role to which he was so eminently suited, acting the wise older statesman, criticising the Thatcher Government's economic policies and especially privatisation as equivalent to "selling the family silver", not the most penetrating analogy for the huge majority of families which had no family silver to sell.

SuperMac, especially when complete with the glasses that Macmillan never wore in public, was meant to be an ironic comment on someone who was not Superman. But if anything it had the opposite effect – a common problem with irony when not understood. Other more obvious aspects were also cartooned – hair, moustache, hats and clothes.

Victor Weisz 'Vicky'
Evening Standard
6 November 1958

Timothy Birdsall
The Drawings of
Timothy Birdsall
M Frayn and B Gascoigne
(1964)

147

Bill Papas
The *Guardian*
1960

Marc Boxer 'Marc'
Britannia Bright's
Bewilderment
by Clive James (1976)

Ken Sprague
Daily Worker

"PARTING IS SUCH SWEET SORROW"
—*Romeo and Juliet, Act II Scene II*

Victor Weisz 'Vicky'
Evening Standard
1963

Michael Cummings
Daily Express
1963

David Low
The Manchester Guardian
31 October 1956

TED HEATH – THE PRAGMATIC CONSERVATIVE

The Conservatives moved as far as they could from the social origins of Alec Douglas Home by electing Ted Heath as Leader in 1965. His father was a carpenter and his mother a maid; he won scholarships to take him to Grammar School and Oxford. Presumably he acquired his plummy middle class voice at Oxford and in the Army where he finished the war as a Lieutenant Colonel. Chief Whip under Eden, middle ranking Minister under Macmillan, his main success had been abolishing retail price maintenance, an unpopular decision amongst many Conservatives. With Macmillan he led the unsuccessful attempt to negotiate Britain into Europe. But he had held none of the top three jobs when, in Opposition, he beat ex-Chancellor Maudling in the first competitive vote for a Conservative leader. The Party wanted an abrasive answer to Wilson, but did not realise he lacked Wilson's devious dexterity.

He was not seriously blamed for defeat in the 1966 General Election, and received surprised praise for achieving an unexpected win in 1970. In between he carried out what many outside the Conservative Party regarded as his greatest act, when he sacked Enoch Powell from the Shadow Cabinet in 1968. His success in taking the United Kingdom into Europe in October 1971 was seen by some Conservatives then as a betrayal – and the number of critics grew in vehemence over the next 30 years. He had gone into the Election of 1970 with a Conservative programme of lowering taxes and removing burdens on industry. In government he decided that changed circumstances required changed policies, so some 'lame ducks' were supported, and he introduced incomes policies. His was essentially a pragmatic approach, driven by what he hoped would work rather than by dogmatic adherence to Conservative principles.

Problems with the still powerful miners' trade unions led to strikes, a three-day working week and the threat of an economic meltdown. He called a General Election in February 1974, posing the question: 'who governs?' The answer was 'someone else'. A despairing attempt to agree a coalition with Jeremy Thorpe and his small Liberal Party did not succeed but lowered his reputation as a man of stern principle. The General Election loss of October 1974 was his third in four attempts, but he was nonetheless surprised when Conservative MPs took advantage of a new procedure that allowed a challenge to him as leader. He was even more surprised when Margaret Thatcher became the main challenger, and was astonished and permanently angered by her success in February 1975. He remained permanently in opposition to her, stubbornly staying in the House of Commons for 26 years after his replacement as leader. He seemed to take pleasure in his relationship with her being described as "the longest sulk in political history". He was especially angered by her relationship with Europe but also by her economic policies. Thatcherites portrayed him as someone who surrendered Conservative principles in a u-turn from 1972, and who personally had not a chip but a log on his shoulders. He became a more effective speaker in his older age than he had been as Prime Minister, with occasional sorties into a dry wit. When Thatcher was removed in 1990 he denied that he had said "rejoice, rejoice". He claimed he had said "rejoice, rejoice, rejoice".

His deployment of political skills in dealing with people as a politician was extremely selective. For every person who had gone beyond his gruff exterior to engage in a meaningful conversation, there were ten with whom he engaged in no conversation at all, especially women.

He was a gift to cartoonists because of physical characteristics and because of his outside interests – music and sailing. Also his gleaming teeth – exposing his smile was a constant reference point. His physical expression of reaction to a joke, shaking shoulders, was also featured. Like Margaret Thatcher's hats this latter became out of date, and was sometimes replaced by an inaccurately long nose.

While many politicians have some cartoons on their walls, Heath created a gallery devoted to political cartoons (mostly of himself) at his house in Salisbury. Around 50 are on show at any one time.

Victor Weisz 'Vicky'
Evening Standard
July 1965

John Kent
Private Eye
24 September 1971

Wally Fawkes 'Trog'
The *Observer*
31 October 1971

'I was going to ask about all that technological know-how Britain will bring into Europe.'

Wally Fawkes 'Trog'
The *Observer*
20 February 1972

Marc Boxer 'Marc'
*Britannia Bright's
Bewilderment*
by Clive James (1976)

Michael Cummings
Daily Express
8 June 1973

John Jones 'Jon'
Daily Mail
5 March 1974

155

MARGARET THATCHER – THE RADICAL CONSERVATIVE

"No woman in my time will be Prime Minister or Chancellor of the Exchequer or Foreign Secretary. Anyway I wouldn't want to be Prime Minister." Thus spoke Margaret Thatcher, a middle-ranking shadow minister in October 1969. When her Cabinet Ministers' "treachery with a smile on its face" pushed her out in 1990 she had won three General Elections and been Prime Minister for 11 years.

The combination of family background (father a small shopkeeper) education (Grammar school and Oxford), professional training (scientific research and the law) made her into the person and Prime Minister she became. One of only 12 women Tory MPs in 1959 her gender was then a disabling rather than the enabling feature it would have been in the 21st century. As a female Prime Minister she seems to have gained some benefits from the uncertainties of men in dealing with a woman who was in every sense their superior. She was however, though a beacon of achievement for women, not a role model.

She acquired her first major fame as Secretary of State for Education in the Heath government, where she removed the entitlement to free school milk from some children and famously agreed to the ending of more Grammar schools in favour of Comprehensives than her Labour predecessors. Unlike Tony Benn she did not voice in Cabinet her disagreement with those policies that she later condemned as part of the failed consensus post-1945 policies. She had the courage to stand against Heath in the leadership election of 1975, and MPs desperate to replace him, even with a woman, elected her in the second ballot. This was her first major piece of luck. Thereafter her career was studded with further pieces of good fortune, which she turned to her advantage in advancing the particular kind of reactionary but radical conservatism which she gradually espoused. Gradually, because neither in 1975 nor in the 1979 General Election did she espouse the kind of Thatcherite programme that she developed in government. She had the good luck to be available when the winter of discontent in 1979 finally finished off the Labour government, of which she had not been a particularly successful opponent. But the early actions of her Government made her and it very unpopular until the Falklands War. To fight it was a tremendous gamble, which, unlike Eden, she won. Good luck continued with the collapse of Labour with Foot and Benn, the creation of the Social Democratic Party and finally the arrival of the ranting hard Left ideologue, Arthur Scargill, to initiate a miners' strike. As it turned out her final piece of luck was to be in the right room at the right time when the IRA bomb exploded in her hotel suite in Brighton in October 1984.

Good luck served her policies. North Sea oil paid for the unemployment created by her economic policies. Her belief in market economics and the academic tenets of monetarism caused the unemployment. Privatisation and the sale of council houses provided her with more money through which she lowered taxes and created more shareowners and homeowners. A succession of trades union reform laws, and large-scale unemployment muted the trades unions.

Those people in work felt the benefit of reduced direct taxes, providing they were not affected by the reduction in the range and quality of public services. In foreign affairs she created an image of a restored Great Britain with close relations with the United States. She turned her luck into a transformation of British society.

Prime Ministers are expected to be authoritative – why else are they there? Yet Thatcher became authoritarian. While her fans said that she was always willing to participate in a good argument, others felt this was increasingly untrue. Her longest serving Cabinet Minister, Geoffrey Howe, on his resignation thrust in the dagger and a large minority of MPs voted against her in the subsequent leadership election. Only two 20th Century Conservative leaders left entirely of their own volition – Salisbury and Baldwin. Thatcher's was the most public humiliation of all those who had been pushed out.

Cartoonists drew different Thatchers – admirers portrayed her as Joan of Arc and an Iron Lady, critics as manic or maniac. Scarfe said that in his drawings "she turned from flesh and blood into pure polished dangerous unyielding, crushing, cutting metal". But Wally Fawkes 'Trog' tried to draw her as vapid, vain and wrong.

According to Kenneth Clarke on opening a Political Cartoon Society exhibition on Thatcher entitled 'Handbagged' in 2002, she "was the greatest gift to political cartoonists since Churchill. It's not just the handbag. You walk in here, take one look at her nose and people like me suddenly grow pale".

left
Michael Cummings

right
Marc Boxer 'Marc'
This was Margaret Thatcher
when Secretary of State for
Education

Wally Fawkes 'Trog'

Gerald Scarfe
1983
This cartoon, together with one
of Nigel Lawson, also by Scarfe,
was bought by the National
Portrait Gallery for £4,510 in
October 1988.

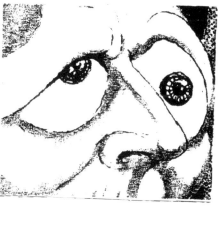

Steve Bell
Bell discovered that one of
Thatcher's eyes was hooded.

Charles Griffin

Kevin Kallaugher 'KAL'
The Economist
1985

Nick Garland
Independent Magazine
29 December 1990

CHAPTER 12
PERSONALITIES

INTRODUCTION

Roy Hattersley wrote in 2001 that "politics should be primarily concerned with principles, policies and programmes". It is difficult to cartoon a policy, so cartoonists often focus on personalities. Earlier chapters inevitably highlighted Prime Ministers. This chapter captures individuals who were significant in the history of the Conservative Party or were of special interest to me as an observer of political life.

NANCY ASTOR

Women secured the right to become an MP, and a majority of them the right to vote, following the Representation of the People Act of 1918. Nancy, Lady Astor, became the first woman to take her seat when she was in effect given the Plymouth Sutton seat by her husband when he became a Viscount in 1919. As a Conservative MP from that date until 1945 she was more liberal on social affairs than most Conservatives, but also in the 1930s a dedicated appeaser of Nazi Germany. The Cliveden Set that she was supposed to lead from her house on the Thames was an invention, however, by Claude Cockburn, a left wing journalist. She was also a dedicated teetotaller and presented her views vigorously both in public meetings and in the House of Commons, securing a drinking age limit of 18. Her exchanges with Winston Churchill, not a teetotaller, both apocryphal and actual, added to her reputation.

Bert Thomas
Meet These People by R Arkell
(1930)

LORD BIRKENHEAD

F E Smith first developed his reputation at Oxford, then as a coruscating barrister unafraid of offending judges, before becoming an MP in 1906. He admired his own brilliance of mind even more than did his friends. Margot Asquith said "his brains have gone to his head". It was not the fact that he was so clever which offended people and led to distrust, but his constant exhibition of his intellect and powers of expression. His enemies, particularly those offended by his wit, focused on self-indulgence. His early career in the Commons developed from a brilliant maiden speech and further attacks on Liberal legislation. His fame arose from his vehement support of Ulster and Irish Home Rule. After the War as Lord Chancellor in Lloyd George's Coalition he pushed the reform of the divorce laws, and assisted Lloyd George both in reaching agreement with the embryonic Irish Republic and also selling partition to Ulster.

In 1923, in a speech to students at Glasgow University, he made comments that represent brilliantly an aggressive strand of Conservatism, such as "the world continues to offer glittering prizes for those who have stout hearts and sharp swords".

A *New Statesman* cartoon by David Low portrayed F E Smith as 'Lord Burstinghead', much to F E's dissatisfaction. In his autobiography Low said he was aiming at the fact that F E "never concealed his superiority". He made no reference to the impact of alcohol on F E's head. This was never explicitly referred to publicly, unlike comments about George Brown in the 1960s. The cartoon by Quiz brilliantly captures F E's arrogance.

Powys Evans 'Quiz'
Saturday Review
22 September 1923

ROBERT BOOTHBY

MP for East Aberdeenshire from 1924–1958, he was Parliamentary Private Secretary to Churchill as Chancellor of the Exchequer from 1926–1929. He became a critic of the National Government's economic policies and then of the appeasement of Nazi Germany in the 1930s. He was one of the 41 who voted against Neville Chamberlain in the crucial debate in May 1940. Given a junior job by Churchill, he was forced out of office over a minor previous mistake in not 'declaring an interest'. Despite their previous relationship and Boothby's association with him in the small group before the war, Churchill made no effort to hold on to him. He never achieved office again but developed a huge public reputation through appearances on the then new TV political panels, and on Radio's *Any Questions*. Deep voiced, eloquent, and independent, he was an easy Conservative for opponents to like. In those more restrained times his long affair with Harold Macmillan's wife was not part of his public image.

R A BUTLER

In May 1930 Butler wrote a letter to *The Times* about Harold Macmillan, who had just lost his seat in Parliament, advising him to seek a "pastime more suited to his talents than politics." Macmillan had his revenge in 1957 and 1963.

Butler was one of the many appeasers retained by Churchill in 1940, and later he received promotion to become responsible for education. There he devised the major reform in 1944, extending the right to secondary education to every child. He was the prime mover after the war in the rehabilitation of the Conservative Party through changes in its economic and social policy, and was initially a successful Chancellor of the Exchequer from 1951. He deputised for Churchill and later for Eden as Prime Minister but when 'soundings' were taken when Eden resigned in 1957, Macmillan emerged as the choice of the Cabinet in preference to Butler, whose ambiguous views about the Suez War played against him. Macmillan would not give him the Foreign Office and instead loaded him with a variety of responsibilities for the Home Office and Africa, which ensured unpopularity amongst many Tory MPs. Macmillan, determined that Butler should not be Prime Minister, successfully pushed for Lord Home to succeed in 1963. Butler might have prevented this, by refusing to serve under Home and thus forcing an offer to be made to himself. Other senior Ministers said they would have joined him, including Enoch Powell who said "we handed him a loaded revolver but he refused to shoot". Butler's view was "one cannot change one's nature". Whether, as Macmillan thought at the time, this displayed the lack of steel necessary in a Prime Minister, or whether Butler really felt that splitting the party was a mortal sin, his chance had gone.

He was a gift to journalists with his capacity in off the record conversations to make remarks capable of more than one interpretation, but he did not say that Eden "is the best Prime Minister we have". He had the disabling characteristic of seeming more devious than he was – the opposite of Macmillan.

Ted Harrison
Modern Elizabethans (1977)

EDWARD CARSON

Dublin born, he was like F E Smith another brilliant Conservative lawyer. He reached fame by destroying Oscar Wilde in cross-examination. Despite being a lawyer and therefore presumably obliged to obey the rule of law, he rose to political fame by his enthusiastic support of armed militant and possibly seditious activities in Ulster in support of the majority desire to stay out of a Home Rule Ireland. "I rely on you to keep your arms with a view to keeping the peace", he said to a Regiment of the Ulster Volunteer Force in 1914. He was the Parliamentary leader, with Bonar Law, of the expression of views that took the defence of Ulster's rights beyond the legitimate extreme. The traditional Conservative reverence for law and order clearly, for him, applied to Suffragettes, not Ulstermen.

He was briefly an unsuccessful Minister in the Lloyd George Coalition, and never accepted the results of the 1922 Agreement for Ireland.

Tom Titt
Caricatures (1913)

AUSTEN CHAMBERLAIN

Austen had one relatively brief period of success as Foreign Secretary when he negotiated the Locarno Treaty in 1925. His career was bedevilled by assertions – quite correct – that he was of nothing like the same stature as his father Joseph. He had been successful within the Unionist Party to the level of being the obvious choice as leader when Balfour resigned in 1911. However, it seemed he and Walter Long had in fact much the same support amongst MPs, and it was he who proposed that they should both stand aside and allow Bonar Law to become leader. He had been Chancellor of the Exchequer under Balfour, and returned to that job in 1919 under Lloyd George. Chamberlain favoured Lloyd George's suggestion of 'fusion', ie a merger of the Conservative and Liberal parties, and later as leader of the party, declined Lloyd George's offer to stand aside for him as Prime Minister. In 1922 came his further act of self-abnegation. When at the Carlton Club meeting he found the majority of his party were unwilling to go into a General Election with Lloyd George, he resigned the leadership and twice declined the offer of a post under Bonar Law. He, rather than Stanley Baldwin, would have been the more obvious successor to Law in 1923. When suggestions that Baldwin would bring Chamberlain back into Government in 1935 turned out to be unfounded, Winston Churchill said of Austen: "Poor man, he always plays the game and never wins it."

Like his father, he used a monocle, a helpful tab of identity for cartoonists. Low refused to let him remove it when drawing him.

Bert Thomas
The World (1919)

LORD RANDOLPH CHURCHILL

After the first Duke of Marlborough, the Churchills had been wholly without political distinction until the arrival of Lord Randolph, a younger son of the 6th Duke of Marlborough as MP for Woodstock (the Marlborough village) in 1874. He first acquired fame when with three others, the 'Fourth Party', he sustained a running battle against their own leader in the House of Commons, Stafford Northcote. A splendid platform orator, he described himself as a believer in Tory democracy without managing to attach any particular meaning to that phrase. As Secretary of State for India he opposed coercion there, but became particularly passionate on the issue of sustaining the traditional relationship with Ireland. He "played the Orange Card" by saying that "Ulster will fight, Ulster will be right" in May 1886. Appointed by Lord Salisbury as Leader of the House of Commons and Chancellor of the Exchequer he sought to find money by cutting the

defence budget. So unpopular had he become as a Cabinet colleague that when he submitted his resignation, not really believing it would be accepted, Salisbury did so without any discussion.

Although he remained in the House of Commons, his performances there gradually deteriorated in parallel with his health. The relatively short period of his real fame would by now have little relevance if it were not for two things: the first was the biography by his son Winston, which successfully rehabilitated him as an important Conservative; the second derives from his resignation. He is constantly produced as a reminder for Ministers that they should not threaten resignation unless in so powerful a position that it could not possibly be accepted.

Francis Carruthers Gould
Truth
25 December 1891

ALAN CLARK

Clark started life with all the advantages of Eton, Oxford and a famous, rich father (Sir Kenneth Clark). In 1961 he published *The Donkeys*, a well-written, savage and unbalanced attack on the conduct of the First World War by the generals in France. As an MP from February 1974, it took some time for him to reach even the lower levels of Government, and he remained essentially too unreliable to be given the Cabinet post he craved under the leader he adored. When evidence suggested that he had not told the full story in presenting evidence in an important trial he delivered the supercilious statement that he had been "economical with the *actualité*". The fact that his evidence might have led to someone going to prison did not seem to have bothered him.

Alan Clark's public performances helped to generate the view that he was one of the more dislikeable Conservatives of his time, a view well supported by the diaries he published covering his life as an MP and middle-rank Minister. Those diaries, full of revelations about political life and his own sexual adventures, were a publishing sensation. As with all diaries they represent a version of what the writer chose to record, and in his case almost certainly knowing that they would be published.

John Springs
The Daily Telegraph
8 March 1993

LORD CURZON

In the 19th century Prime Ministers were frequently members of the House of Lords rather than the Commons. Curzon was one of the two peers (the other being Halifax) who, after the Marquis of Salisbury in 1902, might have become Prime Minister as peers (unlike Home) but did not. His time as a reforming Viceroy of India was followed by strong participation in the battle in the House of Commons over Asquith's Parliament Bill. It was he who advised the Party "to fight in the last ditch" against it. But he changed his mind when Asquith revealed he had George V's promise to create sufficient peers if necessary to pass the Parliament Bill.

He was raised to unexpected prominence as one of five members of the War Cabinet under Lloyd George and actually opposed Balfour's declaration about the future of Palestine. He became Foreign Secretary under Lloyd George in October 1919 but 'under' was very much the word. He remained Foreign Secretary under Bonar Law because at the Carlton Club in October 1922 he had opposed Austen Chamberlain over staying with Lloyd George. When Bonar Law resigned as Prime Minister in 1923, Curzon expected to be made Prime Minister, since Austen Chamberlain had effectively ruled himself out.

Powys Evans 'Quiz'
Saturday Review (1923)

THE MARQUESS CURZON OF KEDLESTON, K.G.

There were many stories about his detachment from the ordinary world. When seeing some soldiers bathing he said, "I did not know the lower orders had such white skins". His claim that the "best work in the world was always done by members of the aristocracy", may in some sense have survived in Macmillan's support of Lord Home in 1963.

MICHAEL HESELTINE

Heseltine's decision to stand against Margaret Thatcher after Geoffrey Howe's speech in 1990 provided the means by which Tory MPs disposed of her. Since his departure from the Cabinet in 1986 he had long proclaimed that he did not scc the circumstances in which he would stand against her – but now the circumstances had arrived. He did not receive the ultimate reward, since John Major went on to beat him in the second election.

He was a fascinating politician. He had built up his own wealth principally through his publishing company. He took into his ministerial jobs some of the managerial disciplines from that company. He hit the headlines in 1976 when he lifted the Mace in the House of Commons – he said as a gesture of contempt at the Labour Party breaking rules. A succession of oratorical triumphs at Conservative Party conferences where he was able to savage the Labour Party were accompanied by real concern for the problems in inner cities, expressed particularly through his efforts to regenerate Liverpool. Always prepared to abuse 'socialists', in practice he was prepared to intervene against the excesses created by monetarism. The difference of opinion he had with Margaret Thatcher over Westland Helicopters in 1986, revolving around his commitment to Europe and distaste for her approach to managing the dispute, led to his literally walking out of Cabinet. John Major cuddled him close in 1990, making him Deputy Prime Minister. A heart problem removed any temptation to stand for the Conservative leadership in 1997.

Cartoonists, especially Steve Bell, created an image of Heseltine as Tarzan, following earlier representations based on him swinging the Mace. They also fixed on the glowing blonde mane of hair, carefully tended for effect.

Wally Fawkes 'Trog'
Observer Magazine
9 October 1989

KEITH JOSEPH

"It was only in April 1974 that I was converted to Conservatism. I had thought that I was a Conservative but now I see that I was not one at all". This was Joseph's reappraisal of his experiences as a minister under Ted Heath, when both in relation to Housing and Social Services his departments spent large sums of money. As with other kinds of convert, Joseph's new espousal of the doctrines of Frederick Hayek, and his belief in Friedman's economic doctrine of monetarism made a profound break with what is now called the post-war Consensus. Margaret Thatcher said that Joseph was the real architect of Thatcherism – indeed she too had followed the normal Conservative line when Secretary of State for Education under Heath. But Thatcher did not immediately engage in such a dramatic disavowal of her past.

Joseph would have been the candidate of those who wanted to break with corporate conservatism when Heath was forced to put himself up for re-election. But Joseph, already seen by some colleagues as a potential disaster, ruled himself out following the media furore over a speech he made in October 1974. Part of it was wholly acceptable – the need somehow to disrupt the cycle of deprivation which perpetuated the problems of the lowest social classes. His suggestion that the cycle should be broken by reducing the number of children born to these classes turned into an accusation that he was a believer in eugenics. Thatcher stepped into the role as an alternative to Heath and became leader. Although she admired Joseph and continued to welcome his ideas, she did not make him Chancellor. Nor was he a great success as a senior Cabinet Minister under her, continuing to be accident-prone.

Cartoonists made use of his tortured facial expression as he grappled with the complexities of the arguments he advanced. They also made use of a Conservative description of him – quite inaccurate – as 'the mad monk'.

Marc Boxer 'Marc'
Britannia Bright's
Bewilderment by Clive James
(1976)

IAIN MACLEOD

Macleod was given early office under Winston Churchill in May 1951. This resulted from the accident of Churchill being in the House of Commons chamber when Macleod made a verbal assault on Aneurin Bevan. He said he proposed to deal with relish with Bevan's "vulgar, crude and intemperate speech". He was the last great Conservative orator, a performer whose skill in part lay in concealing how much technique was going into his speech. He differed from Michael Heseltine in the extraordinary tonal quality of his voice, in being equally effective in the Commons and at conference, and in the fact that he was sometimes speaking against Conservative traditional opinion. Although in fact a social reformer in beliefs – one of the founders of the 'one nation' group - he was always prepared to exaggerate in biting phrases the distance between himself and the Labour Party.

Macmillan made him Colonial Secretary in 1959, and in that job he accelerated the process of giving independence to British Colonies. Sneered at by the right-wing Marquis of Salisbury as being "too clever by half" Macleod did what he thought right, though it produced permanent disfavour amongst many Conservatives. It was to the Tory conference in October 1961 that he said, "I believe quite simply in the brotherhood of man – men of all races, of all colours, of all creeds." His actions in the Colonial Office gave practical expression to this belief, and in 1968 he opposed a Labour Government race based Immigration Act.

He further showed he was prepared to pay the price of his beliefs when he refused to serve under Lord Home, whom he thought a wholly inappropriate choice as Prime Minister in 1963. He later published an article in the *Spectator* magazine decrying both the process through which Home had 'emerged', and the actual numbers supposedly supporting him. He later returned to the Shadow Front Bench but had only a few weeks as Shadow Chancellor of the Exchequer before his early death.

Cartoonists made the best they could of a bald head and relatively bushy eyebrows. I have found only one cartoon that showed his very badly deformed shoulder and back.

Victor Weisz 'Vicky'
Evening Standard
1965

ENOCH POWELL

"Those whom the gods wish to destroy, they first make mad. We must be mad, literally mad, as a nation to be permitting the annual inflow of some 50,000 dependants. I am filled with foreboding. Like the Roman, I seem to see 'the River Tiber foaming with much blood.'" Iain Macleod's view was "Poor Enoch – driven mad by the remorselessness of his own logic." Following that speech on 20 April 1968, Heath sacked him from the Shadow Cabinet. Although he retained prominence as a public figure, and was admired at least for his economic views – a version of monetarism – by Margaret Thatcher, his substantial career ended following that speech. There was no question of him serving under Heath from 1970 and after resigning his seat and advocating a vote for Labour; he finished his political life bizarrely as an Ulster Unionist MP.

It was the combination of the cerebral and the emotional which made him a very effective public speaker. He was a man of unwavering self-belief, which enabled him to speak and act on the principles that he developed for himself. He was one of the three Treasury Ministers who resigned from Macmillan's Government in 1958, and he joined with Macleod in refusing to serve under Home. He thought Butler, with whose economic views he differed, would nonetheless be a better Prime Minster. He secured a derisory number of votes – 15 – in the 1965 leadership election and was an uncomfortable colleague before Heath sacked him for the speech. There was undoubtedly an issue to be discussed – but Powell sullied his argument by references to 'picaninnies', blood and excrement through letterboxes. His intemperate forecasts were not borne out. He opposed Bills on discrimination against women and race discrimination, which he saw as affronts to individual liberty. Powell had said in his own biography of Joseph Chamberlain, "All political lives unless they are cut off in mid-stream at a happy juncture end in failure". It is not clear what the happy juncture might have been for him.

John Jensen
On the House by Simon Hoggart (1981)

BIBLIOGRAPHY

BOOKS ON CARTOONS AND CARTOONISTS

K Baker *The Prime Ministers* Thames & Hudson 1995

S Bell *Bell's Eye* Methuen 1999

T S Benson *Low and Lord Beaverbrook* Unpublished Phd Thesis 1998

T S Benson Low on Churchill in *Churchill in Caricature* Political Cartoon Society 2005

T S Benson *Strube* Political Cartoon Society 2004

T S Benson *The Cartoon Century* Random House 2007

W S Churchill Cartoons and Cartoonists in *Thoughts and Adventures* Macmillan 1932

M Cummings *On the Point of My Pen* Milestone 1985

R Davies & L Ottaway *Vicky* Secker & Warburg 1987

A Gould *The Picture Politics of Francis Carruthers Gould* in *20th Century Studies* 1975

J Jensen *"Curious! I seem to hear a Child Weeping"* (Will Dyson) in *20th Century Studies* 1975

D Low *Ye Madde Designer* Studio 1935

F Morris *Artist of Wonderland* (John Tenniel) Lutterworrth Press 2005

A Mumford *Stabbed in the Front* University of Kent 2001

A Mumford *Did Cowards Flinch?* Political Cartoon Society 2006

C Press *The Political Cartoon* Associated University Presses 1981

G Scarfe *Drawing Blood* Little, Brown 2005

C Seymour Ure Prime Ministers and Political Cartoons in *Prime Ministers and the Media* Blackwell 2003

C Seymour Ure *What Future for the British Political Cartoon* Journalism Studies Vol 2 No2 2001

C Seymour Ure & J Schoff *David Low* Secker and Warburg 1985

F Urquhart *WSC A Cartoon Biography* Foreword by H Nicolson Cassell 1955

HISTORY OF THE CONSERVATIVE PARTY

R Blake *The Conservative Party from Peel to Major* Heinemann 1997

A Clark *The Tories: Conservatism and the Nation State 1922-1997* Phoenix 1998

A J Davies *We The Nation* Abacus 1996

J Ramsden *An Appetite for Power* Harper Collins 1999

G Wheatcroft *The Strange Death of Tory England* Allen Lane 2005

GENERAL HISTORY

M Bentley *Politics without Democracy 1815-1914* Blackwell 1999

P Clarke *Hope and Glory* Penguin 1997

P Clarke *A Question of Leadership* Hamish Hamilton 1991

P Hennessy *Never Again* Jonathan Cape 1992

P Hennessy *Having It So Good* Allen Lane 2006

R R James *The British Revolution 1880-1939* Methuen 1978

J Ramsden *The Oxford Companion to Twentieth Century British Politics* Oxford University Press 2002

A Watkins *The Road to Number 10* Duckworth 1998

The series of books on General Elections since 1945, first OUP then Macmillan.

BIOGRAPHIES

The Dictionary of National Biography 2004 has been a primary but never sole source. Some contributions (as with the Oxford Companion mentioned above) are distinctly one-sided. Of the biographies and autobiographies studied, the following were the most interesting

RJQ Adams *Balfour: The Last Grandee* John Murray 2007

RJQ Adams *Bonar Law* John Murray 1999

R Aldous *The Lion and the Unicorn: Gladstone vs Disraeli* Hutchison 2006

S Ball *The Guardsmen* Harper Collins 2004

A Horne *Macmillan 2 vols* Macmillan 1988, 1989

A Howard *R A B the Life of R A Butler* Jonathan Cape 1987

D Hurd *Robert Peel* Weidenfeld & Nicolson 2007

R Jenkins *Churchill* Macmillan 2001

E Pearce *The Lost Leaders* Little, Brown 1979

D R Thorpe *The Uncrowned Prime Ministers* Dark Horse Publishing 1980

D R Thorpe *Eden* Chatto & Windus 2003